Come On Along
& Listen to

My
Life in
Theatre

Come On Along & Listen to My Life in Theatre

written by **Martin Markinson**

ARCHWAY
PUBLISHING

Archway Publishing books may be ordered through booksellers or by contacting:

Archway Publishing
1663 Liberty Drive
Bloomington, IN 47403
www.archwaypublishing.com
1 (888) 242-5904

Because of the dynamic nature of the Internet, any web addresses or links contained in this book may have changed since publication and may no longer be valid. The views expressed in this work are solely those of the author and do not necessarily reflect the views of the publisher, and the publisher hereby disclaims any responsibility for them.

Any people depicted in stock imagery provided by Getty Images are models, and such images are being used for illustrative purposes only. Certain stock imagery © Getty Images.

ISBN: 978-1-4808-7631-6 (sc)
ISBN: 978-1-4808-7632-3 (hc)
ISBN: 978-1-4808-7630-9 (e)

Library of Congress Control Number: 2019906645

Print information available on the last page.

Archway Publishing rev. date: 6/7/2019

I dedicate this memoir to my beautiful wife and lifelong companion, Arlena Markinson, to our wonderful children – Brett & Alison, Keith & Lisa, our daughter Sydney, and to our beloved grandchildren – Jade, Jasmine, Luke, and Bennett.

In Fond Memory of
Donald Tick, my friend and business partner for over 40 years.

Acknowledgements

I wish to express my heartfelt gratitude to the following people – all of whom played a starring role in helping to bring this book into being: My magnificent wife, Arlena Markinson; Susan Myerberg, my house counsel and general manager of the Helen Hayes Theatre for 35 years; George Cappannelli, dear friend and major instigator of this memoir; Jann Arrington-Wolcott whose first novel propelled me into the world of motion picture production; and Laurel Airica, the book editor recommended to me by George who has helped me tell my story in ways we hope will entertain, inform and possibly inspire the reader.

Table of Contents

Part V: The Final Curtain

Part VI: Encore!

Part VII: Appendices

Letter from the Editor

"If the single man plant himself indomitably on his
instincts, and there abide, the huge world will come
round to him."   Ralph Waldo Emerson

As you soon will read, Marty Markinson has lived an extraordinary
life. His memoir is what people used to call 'a real Horatio Alger
Story'. For in those 19th C novels by Horatio Alger, Jr., Marty rose
from modest means and obscurity to wealth, respectability and significant influence through a combination of laudable qualities – including
honesty, courage, grit, creativity, high hopes, positive intentions plus
a lot of hard work. And Marty had fun all the way to the top of his
chosen profession.

When I read through his manuscript for the first time, particular
statements stood out for me because they so clearly illustrated his
philosophy of life. As a student of what is commonly referred to as
the Law of Attraction, which deals with the mental and emotional
outlooks that assist us in bringing about the outcomes we desire, I
saw that throughout his life Marty had been naturally practicing attitudes and behaviors that promote states of well-being and fortunate
circumstances.

As he emphasizes in his memoir, there are no blueprints that
assure success on Broadway – or anywhere else for that matter. Yet,
Marty experienced extraordinary levels of success to a degree that
the giants in the theatre industry – the Shuberts, the Nederlanders
and the Jujamcyns – assured him at the outset were totally impossible.

As the owner of the smallest professional venue on Broadway – in a highly competitive industry – Marty's Little Theatre was rarely dark. And his life in this ego-fueled business was virtually conflict-free because he was so quick to resolve any issues that arose in ways that turned many would-be adversaries into lifelong allies.

Through my own life experiences, I have learned that our habits of mind and attitudes toward each other ultimately have a far greater impact on outcomes – and on our own resiliency – than do our most brilliant strategies. So, even before formally editing his manuscript, I culled from Marty's memoir certain statements that reflect the mental and emotional practices that so clearly contributed to the on-going good fortune he has enjoyed in both his personal and professional life. You will find 'Some of the Secrets of Marty's Success' near the end of the memoir – immediately following Marty's Epilogue.

In my view, Marty's perspective, as reflected in all the pages that follow, is a significant part of the legacy that he is leaving to members of the entertainment industry – and to people on every life path. As you read his story, you will gain a sense of how a good natured, kind-hearted, adventurous and creative spirit can surmount extraordinary obstacles to achieve impossible dreams – whose positive impact blesses millions of people. We hope you enjoy taking this journey with Marty from rags to riches on all levels.

Laurel

Laurel Airica 2018

Foreword

It was a night that changed my life forever: June 5, 1983. Arlena, my wife, and I were at the Uris Theatre in New York City for the 37th Annual Tony Awards. That year, Richard Burton, Lena Horne, and Jack Lemmon hosted the event. The orchestra's Special Salute consisted of a medley of George Gershwin songs beautifully sung by an array of celebrities. Then, at the end of the musical salute, the Uris Theatre was officially renamed the Gershwin Theatre.

My feelings of apprehension were indescribable. We were sitting near the front of the theatre surrounded by the people who helped to make Broadway – Broadway. All of us we were poised to hear the announcement of the winner for Best Play in the 1982-83 season.

My heart was pounding almost out of my chest. I was beyond excited because the show I was producing, *Torch Song Trilogy*, was one of the nominees. Everyone in the theatre industry knew it was a long shot because a show entitled *'night, Mother,* by Pulitzer Prize-winner Marsha Norman, was expected to take the Tony, hands down.

Torch Song Trilogy was a groundbreaker, the first on Broadway to fearlessly embrace the gay world. I was concerned as to whether the theatre industry or the theatre-going public would ever fully accept and embrace this show.

Thoughts and memories flooded my mind. I'd always loved the entertainment business. Growing up, I went to as many movies and plays as I possibly could. But how could I ever have imagined back then that one day I would be sitting at the Tony Awards with a Broadway show that I had produced in the running for a Tony?

When the time came to announce the winner, I happened to glance over at the *'night, Mother* producer and it seemed to me that he was preparing to stand up. Then the presenter opened the envelope, saying, as they always do, "And the winner is ..." She gasped. "Oh, my God! The winner is *Torch Song Trilogy!*"

The audience went wild. I just sat there completely stunned. Then it dawned on me that I was expected to get up and accept the Award with the fabulous *Torch Song* team of co-producers and, of course, the extraordinarily gifted author and star of *Torch Song*, Harvey Fierstein. I leaned over to kiss my wife and ran up the stairs onto the stage.

Even producers who have won multiple Tony Awards remember their first as the most thrilling. For me, it was absolutely over-whelming. I stood there, looking out at the distinguished crowd. The realization that millions of people were watching, including my family, friends and colleagues, caused my knees to shake and my mouth to go dry as a desert.

The *Torch Song Trilogy* magic didn't end there. Harvey won Tony's for Best Writer and for Best Actor in a Play! You can imagine the celebration party that night for Harvey, all the producers, and everyone involved in the play – the entire cast, crew and investors. After I was home, my head still whirling, it was suddenly clear to me that theatre, against all odds, was always meant to be my life's work.

Let me tell you how it all played out.

NOMINATION

ANTOINETTE PERRY AWARD

Best Play-Producer
MARTIN MARKINSON
KENNETH WAISSMAN
LAWRENCE LANE
JOHN GLINES
Bet Mar
DONALD TICK
TORCH SONG TRILOGY
1982-83

The League of New York Theatres and Producers, Inc.
Presented Under Authorization of American Theatre Wing, Inc.

The Antoinette Perry (TONY) Award Nomination 1982-83
Best Play *TORCH SONG TRILOGY*

Arlena and Martin Markinson

The Tony Award for Best Play *Torch Song Trilogy*

Part I

Discovering My Place in the World

Chapter 1
How It All Began

My parents emigrated from Russia and settled in Brooklyn, New York in the early 1900s. My late-in-life appearance in December of 1931 was a big surprise to them and to my four grown siblings.

My eldest sister, Eve, a wife and mother, was 25 years older than me. My next sister, Sally, was 20 years my senior and pregnant with her first child at the same time that my 48-year-old mother was pregnant with me. My brother Irving, 18 years old at the time of my arrival, and my sister Gertrude, who was 16, were both living at home when I arrived but were out of the house by the time I was a toddler.

When my sister Sally suffered the loss of her baby, she and her husband Ben privately discussed the possibility of asking my parents to adopt me. After all, my parents had already been grandparents for five years at that point. Surely, they didn't want to start all over with a baby of their own. Fortunately for me, Sally and Ben decided to adopt a dog instead, so the subject was never broached with my parents. I'm glad for that as I may have found it quite confusing as a child.

Growing up during the Depression, my whole world revolved around Montgomery Street in Crown Heights, Brooklyn. All my

friends lived on this street. And all the stores where we did our shop-
ping were on Montgomery or just around the corner.

School was three blocks from my house. Although I wasn't a good
student, I managed to get through it. Athletics were my real interest,
along with music.

Inspired by the big band sounds that I listened to on the radio,
I planned to be a musician when I grew up. So when I was about
10 years old, I would take the trolley an hour each way to get to my
regular trumpet lessons. When, after a year, it became obvious that I
lacked aptitude for the instrument, the expense of the lessons no longer
felt like a worthwhile investment to my struggling parents.

Managing expenses was a key part of everyday. Around this same
time, when I was about nine years old, my older brother (18 years my
senior) joined the army. Rather than letting his good shoes go to waste
in the closet, my parents put them on me with paper stuffed in the toes,
since the shoes were way too large. Embarrassed but determined, I
greeted my school mates' taunts about my big feet with the reply that
large feet balanced my height!

I had lots of friends and we played ball in the streets while looking out for passing cars. It was a happy life for me despite the fact
that my mother's health was weak and my father was gone six days
a week – until seven or eight at night – working as a sewing machine
repairman.

Everything was hard for them. Yet, I never felt insecure or that I
had an unstable household largely because my adult brother and sisters, who lived nearby, were always so loving toward me. Consequently,
I felt good about myself and was optimistic about my life even after
my father died when I was 11 years old.

My father left behind a small, four-family house for my mother
and me. It was two stories high with two apartments on each floor.
We lived upstairs with our back windows facing the alleyway and
side windows looking out on the four-plex next door. By renting
three of the apartments, my mother was able to cover all of our
expenses. Money, or rather the lack of it, was always a problem
for her. Yet money was never important to me as a kid or even as

an adult. If I had enough money to take care of myself, everything seemed fine to me.

I never dreamed of becoming wealthy or strived to become a millionaire. I had friends for whom having a lot of money was very important. It just was never that important to me. Only the lack of money.

Chapter 2
My Early Career

I got my first job at 12, in 1943, selling copies of *The Sunday New York Times* to people in nearby apartment buildings. Every Sunday morning, a truck would pull up and unload a pile of papers for kids like me to peddle. Whoever showed up took 10 papers at a time and sold them for 25 cents a piece to the people in the neighborhood apartments. We made a penny per copy.

My average sale for a Sunday morning was 25 papers, which bought me two hot dogs and a Pepsi Cola, with 10 cents left over to go to the movies that afternoon. Boy, was that a thrill! My mother had enough income through her tenants that she didn't need me to contribute. So she was happy when I could take care of myself.

At age 13, I changed jobs. A friend-of-a-friend-of-a-relative knew someone in the women's retail shoe business who needed a helper to put shoes back in boxes after customers tried them on – and then put them back into inventory. So, on Saturdays and Sundays I worked in that shoe store for eight hours a day, which severely curtailed my movie-going opportunities.

The summer I was 14, my physically ailing mother wanted to go to Saratoga Springs in upstate New York for the baths and healing mineral waters. Since I needed to be 16 years old to get a job, I lied about my age and became a busboy in one of the local restaurants.

At the end of the summer, my mother decided to move to Florida to avoid the harsh New York winters. So, off we went to Miami Beach – using the rent from our four-family house in Brooklyn to pay for our Florida apartment. I went to school there for a couple of years, supplementing our income by working after school as an usher in one of the local movie theatres.

My sister Eve, who had come to visit us with her daughter – my nine-year-old niece, Lenore – wanted to take my mother out to dinner one evening. So though I was only fifteen years old, she trusted my competence and reliability and asked me to take Lenore with me to work. My shift was from 6-9 pm and Lenore could just sit in a seat and watch the films during that time.

The plan should have worked out perfectly. Lenore loved movies and would be able to see the one that was playing almost twice through before I took her home. When I got home around 9:15pm, I put on my pajamas and got ready to go to bed as I had school the next day. My mother and sister came home shortly afterwards and asked me, "Where is Lenore?"

Oh my God! I had forgotten all about Lenore and left her in the theatre!

I immediately put on my pants and shoes and ran the seven blocks back to the theatre. I was panicked because I knew Lenore didn't have our phone number or address so couldn't possibly find her way back home. I was breathless when I arrived at the theatre – just as the movie ended. Lenore looked at me happily and said, "I got to see the movie twice and I really liked it." All was saved.

After selling newspapers, boxing shoes, bussing dishes and now ushering at a movie theatre, I could see that my career trajectory was rapidly improving. Looking back on the ushering job, I realize that not only was I seeing movies for free, but I was also immersing myself in the art of storytelling and becoming enamored with actors, singers, and dancers. Thus, began my early love affair with the entertainment industry.

I also found my 'mentor' from among the stars. Given that I had no father or any male role model to pattern myself after, I chose Cary Grant. And I began emulating his speech, his gestures and his way of dressing and moving.

After a couple of years in Florida, my mother (now in her sixties) and I moved back to our family home in Brooklyn. Though rentals of the other three units continued to cover most of our expenses, I was approaching 16 and needed to get an after-school job to help make ends meet.

My next job was in a bowling alley, setting pins. This was in 1946, before bowling alleys were mechanized. "Pin boys" would sit on a ledge, and after the first ball was thrown, we'd jump down and clear away the pins that fell. Then, we'd return to the ledge to perch until the second ball was thrown. At that point, we'd step on a lever and little metal pins would pop up, allowing us to reset all the bowling pins by hand for the next bowler.

Up and down, up and down, it was truly backbreaking work that went on until late at night. We received 11¢ per frame, $1.10 per game. And it wasn't steady work. I'd go over after school in hopes they'd have need of me.

In 1947, my 16th year, my mother moved back to Florida for her health. I lived by myself in Brooklyn. And in addition to working to cover my own expenses, I was responsible for taking care of the house with its three other tenant families.

I kept the common areas clean. I took delivery of the coal and made sure the furnace was well stocked and never went out in winter – night or day. The iceman would come several times a week to deliver a big chunk for the icebox in our unit. I made sure to empty the drip pan underneath the icebox so it wouldn't overflow onto the floor. I also collected rents from the three tenants and sent the money to my mother.

Between the need to maintain the house – and to earn an adequate income – it became clear to me that I had to give up something. And that something was my schooling. I had very mixed feelings about quitting two years before graduation. I was embarrassed to tell people or have them find out that I never finished high school.

For several years after, I sometimes felt inadequate around other young people, especially those that went on to college. I kept telling myself, "I had to do what I had to do." Ultimately, I decided to move on with my life and let go of regrets. I needed, somehow, to create a future for myself.

One of my three brothers-in-law was a partner in an insurance agency. In 1947, he got me a full-time job with his agency as a "runner" between the various insurance companies. At that time all the insurance companies were located in close proximity to each other on or around 6 Maiden Lane in Manhattan near Wall Street.

Whenever a client wanted to buy insurance, the agent had to go to an insurance company to purchase it. So as a runner, it was my job to go to the various insurance companies with contracts in hand to obtain a signature so that we knew that the insurance was in place before we gave the policy to the client.

I received the handsome sum of $2/day for my efforts, making a grand total of $12 a week. Back then, that kind of money meant a little something. And I was grateful to have the job, especially considering that the job market was flooded at the time with returning veterans from WWII seeking employment.

Since the insurance business was very conservative, I was expected to wear a suit, jacket and tie. At first, I wore a makeshift jacket that had been sewn for me by my mother. But every week, I was able to put $5 aside. And after three weeks, I went out and bought my first suit and ties – for $15. I already had the white shirts since I'd worn them daily to school.

Since, I didn't want people at work to see me in the same clothes all the time, I invested an additional 50¢ to buy three more ties. Back then, 50¢ was significant money. But the expenditure was well worth it because by rotating my six ties, I had a new look every day of the week.

My $12 weekly salary didn't go very far, of course. I was subsisting on nickel hot dogs and burgers – supplemented by dinners at my sisters with leftovers to take home for the next day's lunch. By the end of a weekend I was always broke except for the bus fare that would get me to one of my three sisters' homes for a decent meal. My three older sisters all lived with their families in various parts of Brooklyn and each one was very happy to feed me. That meant I had three square meals every week.

Happily, I was the apple of my sisters' eyes right from the start. And even when I was 10 and 11 years old and essentially out on my own, I could do no wrong as far as they were concerned. It was because of their big, nurturing hearts that I was such a happy, confident kid – despite the fact that my parents were out of the picture so early in my life.

Not having parents definitely fostered my independence. I taught myself to cook – though nothing as elaborate as what I enjoyed in my sisters' homes. I did my best to stay in touch with my mom when she moved away and to find out how she was doing. However, I couldn't afford to spend much money on long distance calls. So it was almost like all three of my sisters together became my surrogate mother.

Chapter 3
I'm in the Air Force Now

I'd been working in the insurance agency for three years when the Korean War broke out. I was 19-years-old and knew that it was only a matter of time before I would be drafted into the army. So, I decided to enlist in the Air Force for a four-year commitment.

Basic Training was difficult but I was in good shape because I was so athletic. I never had a problem with authority so the discipline didn't faze me. I just did what I had to do without a lot of attitude about it. My closest friends enlisted with me – but they were sent to different places. I felt very lonely for my family.

I was stationed at Stewart Air Force Base in Newburgh, New York. And since my background was in the insurance business I was assigned to the Legal and Claims office. My job was to settle claims for all service men at the base that were involved in automobile accidents, lost luggage and various other types of claims.

After my day of duty was over at 5pm, I was able to get a job at the Officers Club on the base to make extra money as a bartender. That enabled me to buy my first car. It was a 1946 black Pontiac convertible. It needed a lot of work so I got it for very little money. Fortunately, I had friends on the base that worked in the motor pool.

They fixed my car at no cost each time it broke down. All I had to do was drive them around when they needed a ride.

After some time enjoying this quality of military life, I received new orders sending me to Korea. I was somewhat excited that I was going to be involved in the war. However, this excitement quickly vanished and fright took its place when I actually arrived.

The officers in charge looked through my file and saw that I'd been working as a claims investigator. They didn't know what to do with me since there was no such thing as a claims office in a war zone. So, they decided to lend me to the Army Corps of Engineers, which was short of men. Despite all my efforts to avoid it, I was in the Army now!

I was a sergeant at that time and was put in charge of South Korean laborers. We were to go where there were buildings destroyed by the bombings to clear away all the debris and search for any possible survivors.

After many months, when the Army Corps of Engineers got the replacements they needed, I was relieved of my role in Damage Control and reassigned back to my Air Force Command. My new orders reassigned me to the Supply Depot at an air base called K1, located outside of Taegu – a small, unpaved Korean town. Now, my job was helping to deliver the supplies needed at the front lines. I did the loading and unloading of food, clothing and other non-lethal necessities.

It was terrifying. We were always vulnerable to being hit by artillery and bombs. As soon as we unloaded, we turned around and sped back to K1. Almost every night I would think and dream of my family as I was afraid that I would never return home.

I was having lunch one fateful day in the mess hall and sitting next to me was an older Master Sergeant. The war was winding down and peace talks were continuing. He was telling me of his frustration running the Officers Club for several years at an airfield in Korea. Now he was due to return to the States as his tour of duty had ended. But he had to wait until an adequate replacement showed up before he could leave. Unfortunately, none of the potential new replacements had been qualified for his job. When he heard that I had worked at an Officers Club at an air base in the United States, he grabbed me and said, "*You* are going to be my replacement!" It sounded great to me – if I could get the job.

Being that he was a Master Sergeant and had been in the Air Force for many years, he had some pull with his Commanding Officer and built up my resume to include knowing how to run an Officers Club. Thus, he convinced the powers that be that I could be his replacement. And it worked.

I was reassigned from working at the Supply Depot to taking charge of the Officers Club. All the workers at the club – including waitresses, dish washers, and bar tenders – were local Korean people. My job was to supervise their operations and purchase the liquor.

I would fly in to Tokyo to obtain the liquor. I had never been outside of Brooklyn before joining the air force to avoid the draft, so this was another completely foreign culture to me.

It had been only five years since the bombing and surrender of Japan and the country was still undergoing reconstruction. It seemed to me when I rode the train that the other passengers were glowering at me with hostility, which felt scary and uncomfortable. So, I would purchase the liquor for the officers' club from a U.S. military depot and then fly back to Korea the next day without seeing much more of the city or its inhabitants.

It was an unpaid position, of course. But it came with the perk of getting to know some wonderful local Korean people. The most painfully wrenching part of the whole job for me was developing friendships with various pilots who came in to enjoy themselves at night – only to find out soon after that they hadn't returned from their latest missions.

When the war ended I was twenty-two years old and still in Korea. After several months there was an order from President Eisenhower announcing an early release of all enlisted men and women who requested a discharge from the service. It took me several more months to get my early release but I ended up serving a total of three years instead of four.

On the ship coming home to the U.S., I woke up early one morning and watched as we passed under the Golden Gate Bridge. My
heart beat faster and I felt enormous gratitude for my survival.

I hadn't told my relatives that I'd been discharged or that I was
on my way back home. However, I knew from letters they had written
to me that my nephew was getting married at a particular time and
place.

So, I flew home to New York and appeared at the wedding in full
uniform. The shock, relief, crying and hugging, kissing and laughing – enriched one joyous family occasion with another.

The years I spent in the service – including my one-year stint in
Korea – left me with a great deal of confidence in myself and a real
determination to succeed in life. I came out of the Air Force with my
GED – the equivalent of a high school diploma – and with money in
the bank since I had no place to spend the extra pay I received for
serving in a war zone.

Once back in New York, I returned to my old job. Over the next
eight years, I worked hard learning the insurance business and taking
courses in insurance at night. I was convinced that this was going to
be my lifelong profession.

I didn't take advantage of the GI Bill by enrolling in school full
time – in large part because I needed to earn a living. I also felt happy
with who I was and didn't think I needed school to become 'more.'
I knew myself to be clever and resourceful and that worked for me.

Chapter 4
I Meet the Love of My Life

In the summer of 1960, when I was twenty-eight years old, several friends and I decided to rent a house on Fire Island from Memorial Day to Labor Day. We spent every weekend of that entire summer there.

Fire Island is off the coast of New York and is only accessible by ferry. It was a quaint place back then with old beach cottages that were mostly built when life was simpler and relatively quiet. It is known for its beautiful white sand beaches that stretch for miles of unbroken vistas. Only three city blocks wide, Fire Island was also known for the significant flooding that occurred when a bad winter storm would bring the ocean together with the bay.

We would drive out late Friday afternoon after work and return on Sunday evenings. The house we rented was in Ocean Beach. There were a couple of grocery stores, a restaurant and two bars nearby. Nothing more. Transportation was either by bicycle or on foot as no cars were allowed on the island. The idea was total relaxation. Everything was completely casual. We danced the twist to Chubby Checker in the bars at night and went to the movies in a tiny makeshift theatre that was formerly an old meeting hall.

One particular day I was lying on a blanket on the beach with one of my housemates — watching the girls go by. I noticed one of my friends at the water's edge talking to a beautiful girl who looked great in her red and white polka dot bikini. I decided to walk over to see what was going on.

My friend introduced me to Arlena. I was immediately smitten by her beauty and her figure. During our conversation I suggested to my friend that he see if she would like to come over to our house for dinner as we were planning to cook that night. She accepted and came with a friend.

During the course of the evening it was clear to me that I wanted to see Arlena again. I learned that she was twenty-three years old and lived four blocks away from me in Brooklyn. When I found out that she didn't have a ride home lined up for Sunday evening, I offered her a ride with me. She accepted and I was excited — except for the fact that I didn't have a car.

I spent several hours trying to find a ride home before the weekend ended. Luckily, I found someone who was driving with a buddy back to Brooklyn. He offered the back seat of his car to me and my companion.

Once off the ferry and into a car, the ride home took just about an hour. However, it only took a few minutes after Arlena and I got settled into the back seat before we started kissing — and kissing — and kissing — all the way home to her apartment house.

As we started to get out of the car, I noticed that the back window was all fogged up. What a smooch session we had had! Ironically, Arlena's mother and father just happened to be standing out on the sidewalk at the moment we arrived. Thanking my friend for driving us, I told him I would walk the rest of the way back home.

With her lipstick smeared and my face covered with it, Arlena attempted to regain her composure and introduce me to her parents. "Mom, Dad, this is, umm … Um, this is … ". In her embarrassment, she'd forgotten my name. I let her suffer a moment longer then introduced myself.

We dated till the summer of 1961. She then told me that since I had not made a commitment to her, she had decided to take all her money out of the bank and travel to Europe. Perhaps she'd even get a job there.

Not long after that I drove Arlena to the pier where she was leaving from New York. I waved good-bye – not sure of anything at that point. Once in Europe, she called me from time to time. And it was on one of those calls that I realized I was falling in love with her. I was *almost* ready to make a commitment.

After traveling for several months, Arlena returned home with a dollar and change in her bag. I picked her up at the pier and over the next month we got reacquainted. Finally, one evening in a small restaurant in Brooklyn, I proposed marriage to her.

A few months later, on April 15, 1962, Arelena and I were married. She was 25 and I was 30. Though her parents were not wealthy, they were still able to create a small and lovely wedding for us.

We honeymooned in Haiti and Jamaica and then moved into a one-bedroom apartment in Riverdale, New York. Our two sons, Brett and Keith, were both born during our time there. We then borrowed a bit of money from family and were able to buy our first house – in Stamford, Connecticut. A few years later, we welcomed our beautiful daughter, Sydney.

Chapter 5
Insuring Our Future

I became a central part of my brother-in-law's insurance firm as I got to know the clients and enjoyed good relationships with them. Though the insurance business never exactly thrilled me, I had a wife and three children to support along with a mortgage on our home in Connecticut. So, when one of the partners announced his intention to retire, I leapt at the opportunity, borrowed the needed money, and bought out his share of the company.

My nephew, Donald Tick – who was just five years my junior – joined the firm around that time. Together we tripled the business in just a few years by buying out three other insurance agencies and taking care of their clients. One of these agencies primarily handled entertainment insurance for Broadway shows, producers, theatre owners, movies, etc. So, you see where this is heading.

The owner of that agency, Joe Harris, took a liking to me and soon became both a friend and a mentor. A tough old man – about 25 years my senior – he had created his own successful insurance company before becoming a successful producer both on Broadway and in Hollywood.

I admired Joe's dynamic personality and watched how he effortlessly took charge of whatever situation he was in. He would invite me to his home whenever a producer, composer, or playwright was coming over to try out new material on him in hopes that Joe would want to produce their play or musical.

He was very direct and honest with creative people. "I know you can do better than that," he might say to a composer. Or, "this music isn't making it for me." He wasn't always right but you could always trust Joe to give his honest opinion. That was simply the way he conducted business. It was through observing him that I learned to become more diplomatic and honest in sharing my own opinions.

One of the many things I learned from Joe was that you have to put together a really good team when you produce something, or you'll falter down the road. So when I began producing, I made sure that every participant – including writer, director, composer, choreographer, performers, set designer, costume designer, etc. – could work harmoniously with other team members in ways that brought out the best in the material and in each other.

Joe would tell me fascinating and enticing stories about working on Broadway and doing movies in Hollywood. Later on, when I became a producer, he would always invest in my shows – if he liked what I was doing.

One day in 1975, Joe took me to lunch and turned my life around. He told me he was producing a new musical on Broadway, which was being written, directed and choreographed by Bob Fosse, one of the hottest talents of the day. Big-name actors including Gwen Verdon (who was Fosse's wife), Jerry Orbach, and Chita Rivera were signed on to star in the show. It was called *Chicago*.

"Listen, Marty," Joe said, "why don't you come to the meeting, consult on the insurance, raise a little money and join me in producing the show?" My heart gave an excited thump. Oh, wow, I thought. Wouldn't that be interesting!

Chapter 6
My First Foray on Broadway

I invested my own money, contacted friends to raise additional capital, and became part of the team. By listening closely at meetings, I began to learn what went into producing a show.

At one of the meetings, the discussion came around to the actual subject of *Chicago*. All of the producers admitted that the only thing they knew was that Bob Fosse had all the dance and musical ideas mapped out in his head. That's a lot of trust to invest in one person, I thought, no matter how talented he is.

I raised the question as to what we would do if something happened to Fosse. They all just looked at me, not knowing how to answer. I then explained that there was a seldom-used form of insurance called "Abandonment Insurance." And in the event that something devastating happened to Fosse, the policyholder – which was the producing entity – could recover the cost of the show.

At that point the cost of this show, which was $800,000, was mostly already spent. I suggested that we get a quote as to how much this insurance would cost.

When I came back with the quote from the insurance company,

the producers were reluctant to spend the money. However, they finally agreed to purchase it as the premium was quite reasonable.

About three weeks later, the very first day that rehearsals were scheduled to begin, I got a shocking call that Fosse had just suffered a severe heart attack and had been rushed to the hospital. The prognosis was that in three to four months he could probably return to work. The producers wanted to postpone the show for that length of time. But to keep the stars, they would have to pay them their contracted salaries so they wouldn't seek work elsewhere.

I reminded the producers that they could not collect any insurance if they postponed the show – but only if they abandoned it. However, in that case, it could never be redone. They could recoup their $800,000 and return the money to the investors. However, the team believed they had the makings of a hit with Fosse and the cast. So, they didn't want to abandon the show. They then asked if there was anything I could do to keep the show alive.

I went to the insurance company and tried to make a deal, informing them that the producers were ready to abandon the show and collect the $800,000. I suggested that if the insurance company would give the show a $100,000 preferred loan – so that the stars could be paid and the production postponed rather than abandoned – it would be a very good deal for them. They would be saving $700,000; their loan would be paid back as the first priority when the show was up and running' and they would also own a piece of the show.

After several meetings, I was finally successful in convincing the insurance company to take the deal. When Fosse recovered, the rehearsals began. The show went on to become a huge hit and ran for several years, thereby paying back the insurance company and also creating a profit for them and for all the investors.

Chapter 7
Embracing My True Calling

Although I remained in the insurance business, I was now completely smitten with theatre and continued looking for more shows to produce. In the next four years, I produced five more shows on Broadway, one of which was a revival of an old Eddie Cantor show, a 1928 musical comedy called, *Whoopee!*

I first saw that show at the Goodspeed Opera House in Connecticut and immediately loved it. It was a popular theatre, then run by Michael Price, where producers flocked in search of a promising product. Ashton Springer, another New York producer, was also interested in the show. So Price, Springer and I brought *Whoopee!* to Broadway.

Audiences loved it. *Whooppe!* ran for a while and received wonderful reviews. But unfortunately, it never became the hit that we expected it to be. There were few revivals in those days and the feedback was that most people just didn't want to spend money on shows that weren't really new.

During that same period – between 1975 and 1979 – while producing shows on Broadway, I also tried two shows out-of-town and learned about the trials and tribulations of trying to bring a show to Broadway. One of those plays, *The Last Minstrel Show*, was particularly risky. It was the story of the last minstrel show to ever play in a major theatre. The show took place in the1930s in Cincinnati, Ohio.

When minstrel shows were started in the early 19th century, they were a highly racist form of entertainment. White actors in black face would mock people of African descent with jokes, skits, songs and dance. In the 20th C, vaudeville co-opted the variety show format. But minstrel shows continued to be performed on occasion in minor venues – mostly without racist content. Even black entertainers would perform these shows in black face. However, the civil rights movement in the 60s and 70s saw the end of the minstrel show.

The last minstrel show to be performed in blackface on Broadway was in 1909. Our show had an all-African American cast and starred Della Reese. The humor in the show was at no one's expense.

We were in our first week of rehearsals and had a young actor/dancer with a single number in the show. He was so outstanding that by the second week of rehearsals he was given two more big dance numbers. His name was Gregory Hines.

Many people in the Industry, including friends and family of the actors, were very upset upon learning that everyone in the show was applying blackface. This created a great deal of controversy and affected our ability to raise the balance of the money necessary to bring the show to Broadway. Some organizations started to refer to our show as racist.

I decided to call a friend of mine, Ashton Springer, to see the show, give me some advice, and perhaps join me in bringing it to Broadway. Springer was the only African-American producer on Broadway at the time.

He watched a performance, saw too many problems with it, and suggested that I forget about doing this show. So we dropped it. As for the young dancer, Gregory Hines, he was so dynamic that Ashton wanted him for his own Broadway show, *Eubie*. It became a huge hit and propelled Hines to stardom. He went on to do many Broadway shows and to star in movies. It was a loss to the world of entertainment when he died of cancer at the age of 57.

During that same year, a new playwright came to me with a play titled *Dusky Sally*. I was intrigued by the story about the alleged great love affair between Thomas Jefferson and Sally Hemings. A mixed-race woman of great beauty, Hemmings was one of Jefferson's slaves and bore him several children.

Of course, Jefferson's white descendants and most Jeffersonian scholars claimed this was a fable. However, in 1998, DNA tests performed on one of Sally's descendants conclusively confirmed Jeffersonian blood.

The play was set to open in Albany, New York but I felt it needed a lot of changes. I invited some producer friends to come up to see it. They all agreed it needed major rewrites. But when I took my suggestions to the playwright, he refused to change a single word. In the theatre business, even producers can't change a word unless the playwright agrees. So, with all this dissension, I decided to drop the show.

Years later, I heard that the playwright and producer in Philadelphia were sued for plagiarism by the author of the book, *Sally Hemmings*. I still wonder if perhaps the reason the playwright declined to do the necessary work for me was related to the alleged plagiarized excerpts from the novel.

A
Musical Comedy
WHOOPEE!
ASHTON SPRINGER FRANK C. PIERSON MICHAEL P. PRICE
present
WHOOPEE!
Book by
William Anthony McGuire
Lyrics by
Gus Kahn
Music by
Walter Donaldson
starring
CHARLES REPOLE
Associate Producers DONALD TICK and MARTIN MARKINSON
Scenery by
JOHN LEE BEATTY
Costumes by
DAVID TOSER
Lighting by
PETER M. EHRHARDT
Musical Direction by
LYNN CRIGLER
Choreography and Musical Staging by
DAN SIRETTA
Entire Production Directed by
FRANK CORSARO
Originally Produced by the GOODSPEED OPERA HOUSE
ANTA THEATRE

Chapter 8
The Pitfalls of Producing

During my entire career, there were only three other shows that I had to close out of town. Either they didn't work or we ran out of money and couldn't bring them to Broadway.

When I first read the scripts and heard the music for these shows, I felt excited about them. But what sometimes happens when you see a play in action is that it isn't what you had in mind when you read the script.

I had a lot of failures – but it wasn't because the shows weren't good. To be successful on Broadway, you simply have to be a whole lot better than good.

Sometimes, an audience would like a play or musical. However, it would need so many changes that we'd run out of money before we could bring it to the next level. If you don't gauge correctly, it's easy to overspend. And once you have a budget that you have sent out to investors, you can't change it. It's against the law.

You can bring a show in for less money but not for more. If you run short of money and ask for more, individuals can lend you the money as a priority loan. They're then the first ones to get paid back before any of the other investors. Of course, the other investors may not like that. But the choice is that they could lose all their money – or they could make it back as a result of the priority loan. Fortunately, it's very rare that this ever happens.

Here are the three shows that I wasn't able to bring to Broadway.

Nagasaki Dust by W. Colin McKay

I was attracted to this play because I found it interesting and dramatic. It's a very unusual story that gives insight into the life of an American youth of Japanese descent who cannot return home to the U.S.

In this fictional narrative, a Japanese-American student at UCLA learns that his grandmother has died. He travels by ship to Japan for her funeral. While returning to the U.S. on board a Japanese vessel, Pearl Harbor is attacked and the ship he is on must return to Japan.

Though the youth is an American-born citizen, he gets conscripted into the Japanese army against his will. After Hiroshima, the Americans drop leaflets on Nagasaki, warning of another bomb. The student puts all of the American prisoners into an underground torture chamber – as a relatively safe haven – leaving himself exposed. When the war is over, he is tried by the American army as a traitor. Though he is subsequently exonerated, the radiation he had been exposed to eventually proves lethal.

We booked the show for three weeks in Philadelphia to try it out. No critics attended. The audience gave it mixed reviews. So we couldn't take it any further.

Daddy Goodness by Richard Wright and Louis Sapin

This was a fun-loving musical that we again tried out of town. It was about the town drunk who was known as 'Daddy Goodness.' Despite his alcoholism, he had a positive influence on many people and was loved by all. The show wasn't working and the changes we wanted to make to it required new sets and new costumes. Thus, we ran out of money.

Matter of Honor by Michael Chepiga

Playwright, Michael Chepiga read a newspaper article and was intrigued by the story. After researching it, he made the decision to write a play based on events that took place in the 1880s.

The story was about Cadet Johnson Whittaker, the second African-American to be admitted to West Point, who was expelled in his fourth year on a questionable pretext. Approximately 100 years later it was discovered that Cadet Whittaker had been found beaten in his room and after a trial of the assailants, he was wrongly expelled. At a White House ceremony, President Bill Clinton presented to Mr. Whittaker's grandchildren, their grandfather's certificate of graduation as well as his commission.

We presented this play as a tryout at the Pasadena Playhouse in California, to very nice reviews. Unfortunately, we were unable to get the needed financing to take it to Broadway. This play will always linger in my mind and my hope is that someday it will be produced on Broadway. It deserves to be there.

Chapter 9
Becoming a Broadway Theatre Owner

In 1979, I visited Ashton Springer, who had an office in the old, rather dilapidated Little Theatre. It was owned by Westinghouse and located on 44th Street between Broadway and 8th Avenue. Ashton was moving out because the theatre was up for sale. My head started spinning. Oh, my God! What wouldn't I give to own a theatre on Broadway?

I asked Ashton a lot of questions like, "Did they sell it yet? How much do they want? Whom can I talk to?" He didn't have any details but gave me the name of the gentleman handling the deal.

I quickly called to make an offer, saying that whatever the highest offer was, I would offer more. The answer I got from Westinghouse was that the appraised price was set at $800,000; they wouldn't take a penny more or a penny less. There were three offers ahead of mine. Did I want to put my name on the list? The odds were discouraging but I gave them my name – never seriously thinking that I had a chance.

About a week later, on a Friday afternoon, I got a life-changing call from Westinghouse. As it turned out, the first person on the list had wanted to convert the theatre into a restaurant. The theatre industry at the time petitioned Mayor Koch, saying they didn't want to lose a theatre in the area and would he please tell Westinghouse to cease and desist with that offer? The Mayor's office did and they complied.

The second would-be-buyers were a female producer and her husband, a theatrical attorney. As I said, the theatre was a run-down mess. So, after bringing in contractors to determine what work had to be done, they determined that it would cost too much to renovate the place and decided to back out.

The third offer came from two producers of *Annie,* which was running at the time and was a big hit on Broadway. When it came time for closing, however, those producers didn't have enough money and asked Westinghouse to take back a mortgage. Westinghouse refused.

So, the big news was that I, against all odds, was next up. If I wanted the Little Theatre, Westinghouse would need 10% of the total price by Monday – three days away. I ran back to my partner in the insurance business, Donald Tick, telling him I wanted to buy the theatre. He initially thought it was a foolish idea and wasn't interested. I said, "Okay, if you don't want to go in with me, I'll buy it on my own." He reconsidered and we bought it together.

There was no time for an inspection; I had to go with my gut. It didn't matter if it was a terrific price or an inflated one because Westinghouse only gave me three days to make a decision. The 10% down payment was nonrefundable. And the balance of $790,000 was due 30 days later.

Arlena asked me, 'What do you want a theatre for?' I told her that this is a business I like, and I think I'm going to be in this business. So, why wouldn't I want to own a theatre and be part of the small, elite group of theatre owners who controlled Broadway? The decision was easy for me. Now I had my own place.

After the purchase, I decided to visit two prominent people in the theatre business to get their advice. I went first to Jimmy Nederlander, whose organization owned nine theatres on Broadway.

He knew of me because I'd been producing shows on Broadway for the previous four years and had already had a hit. At our meeting, I told him I had just bought the Little Theatre and would greatly appreciate his advice on how I could learn about the way a theatre operates.

Jimmy didn't beat around the bush. "I believe you've made a terrible mistake," he told me. "First of all, with only 500 seats, it's the smallest theatre on Broadway. It's a shit box and will never make any money. There's no way you can compete with me and other theatres owners to bring shows in. And when you don't have a show running, when the theatre is dark, you'll be losing a bundle."

I was so discouraged by his remarks that I was ready to shoot myself. But I reasoned that if I was going to shoot myself, I'd better do it in the foot so I'd still have my head to keep thinking about the mistake I might just have made.

Never one to be easily discouraged, however, I decided to talk to Bernie Jacobs, one of the heads of the huge Shubert Organization, which owned 17 of the 41 Broadway theatres. I sat down with him and repeated what I'd told Jimmy Nederlander. Bernie was a little kinder, but he still told me I was nuts.

I went home that evening and said to myself, "What the heck do I do now? Since I only shot myself in the foot, I still have my brain. And dammit, I am going to make this thing work!"

Even though I now owned the theatre, a play entitled *Gemini*, by Albert Innaurato, was still playing under the Westinghouse licensing agreement – as it had been for the prior three years. Selfishly, I wanted the show to close so we could refurbish the theatre (to the degree we could afford to at that time) and then bring in a new show.

The problem was that *Gemini*'s license with Westinghouse was for very little money so they wanted to stay. Every week, I expected the show to close because they were doing such weak business. However, it was another two years before *Gemini* finally did close – in 1981 – after a five-year run. This was approximately two years after we had purchased the theatre.

The Little Theatre needed extensive and extremely costly

renovations in the neighborhood of $1M. Everything in front of the stage and behind it was in disrepair. So Donald Tick and I decided to start by investing in new seats, new carpeting, new curtains, and new paint. We decided to focus on the backstage areas later.

Chapter 10
Producing My First
In-House Show

Once we made our initial renovations and improvements, we were ready to look for a new show to book. What I quickly learned, however, is that producers weren't interested in coming to a Broadway theatre with only 500 seats. They couldn't make the numbers work to be able to show a profit because theatres typically do most of their business on weekends, and we just didn't have enough seats for the necessary weekend boost. In addition, all producers are sure they have a real hit on their hands so they want a bigger theatre.

At the time I purchased the Little Theatre – and still to this day – three entities controlled almost all of Broadway: The Shubert organization, the Nederlander organization, and the Jujamcyn organization. They are, of course, very competitive. And they all try to find what they think are the best shows available to fill and maintain a long run in their theatres. How in the world could I ever possibly compete with them? I had to find a way.

About that time, I got a call from a producer who asked if I wanted to join him in producing a show called *Ned and Jack* by Sheldon Rosen.

It was a two-character play about an opening-night incident in the life of John Barrymore.

Colleen Dewhurst, a prominent, beloved and extraordinary Broadway actress was making her directing debut with *Ned and Jack*. I was very fond of Colleen as she was a very down-to-earth person, easy to talk to, very active in all phases of theatre, and, of course, loved to act. Colleen lived at the time in upstate New York with her children, chickens and goats. I enjoyed visiting her there.

At the time, *Ned and Jack* was playing off Broadway and the *New York Times* had given it an excellent review. Because the Little Theatre was now dark —and we really needed a good show — I decided to produce it with the caveat that it come to our theatre.

It's a significant undertaking to bring a show from off-Broadway to Broadway. You may have to create all new sets to fit the stage, recast the show, hold rehearsals and advertise. For these reasons, a producer has to decide whether to take the considerable risk of bringing a show to Broadway. With its good reviews I felt very confident that the show was worth the cost and would do well in our theatre.

At the opening night party, the mood was wonderful — that is, until, the reviews came out. When they're bad, it's amazing to see how fast the party empties. In this case, the same reviewer who had given *Ned and Jack* such a good off-Broadway review now implied that it should have never been moved to Broadway. According to him, it just wasn't good enough to make that leap.

There truly are different standards for off-Broadway and on Broadway. These are dictated in part by ticket prices because the greater cost on Broadway necessitates that a show be extraordinarily good. The fact that it can sell out a small theatre and make a profit off-Broadway is no guarantee that it can do so on Broadway.

Colleen was so devastated that I believe she may have cried in the ladies' room until the party was over. It was the first and last time she ever directed.

With no advance sales, I made the decision to close the show on opening night, November 8, 1981, rather than subject Colleen and the other actors to the humiliation of playing to an empty house. When she and I had a chance to reflect after the abrupt closure, she asked me how I felt personally about it.

I told her that ever since I was a very young man, I learned to never get down on myself. Never to lose confidence. I taught myself not to let outside experiences affect the peace and calmness I wanted to feel. I believed if I learned how to handle disappointment, it would be easier to get on in life.

While I was certainly disappointed about the results of the show, I had gone with what I liked because I believed it would work and was willing to take the risk. I was also really happy to be running our own theatre and upgrading it at every opportunity to turn it into a beautiful jewel for entertainers and audiences.

Soon after, in January 1982, I booked *The Curse of an Aching Heart*, into the Little Theatre and attended several rehearsals of the play. Faye Dunaway was in the starring role. And when you have a star, you know you're going to do well.

One scene in the play required Faye to roller skate. It was great fun for me watching the acclaimed actress learn to master this skill on the small stage. The play opened and lasted for about four months. It didn't get great reviews but it made a little money for our theatre – which we immediately poured back into our theatre improvement program.

That show was followed by *Solomon's Child*, a play about people trying to get their son away from a cult. It got mixed or bad reviews and didn't last long, closing toward the end of April 1982.

NED AND JACK

Ken Marsolais, Martin Markinson, All Star Prods. Inc.
and Astral Prods., Inc.
present

NED AND JACK

starring

Peter Michael Goetz
as John Barrymore

John Vickery
as Edward Sheldon

by

SHELDON ROSEN

Directed by

Barbara Schmertz

Setting by
Kevin Griffin

Lighting Designer
James Leonard Joy

Costume Designer
David Murin

Production Stage Manager
Robley Monk

with

Colleen Dewhurst

LITTLE THEATRE

240 West 44th Street

Chapter 11
Learning How to Operate My Theatre Effectively

There's an old saying in the theatre business that it's hard to make a living as a producer but you can make a killing with the right show. I still chuckle when I remember an old-time, very successful producer telling me at this early point in my new career, "Every year you continue to produce on Broadway, you lose one point on your IQ."

I thought about that and decided that I would rather be lucky than smart. Actually, you've got to be a bit of both to succeed.

Another producer cracked me up with his favorite joke: "Do you know what you get when you put a Jew and a homosexual together? You get a Broadway musical!"

Through trial and error I was learning how to be a theatre owner, as well as a producer, and to recognize how to attract shows and producers to my venue. The way a commercial theatre typically operates is that when a producer wants to rent a theatre for his show, the owner asks to see the budget to make sure that the weekly costs to run the show could work out financially at that theatre. In the case of our theatre, with only 500 seats, this was especially essential.

When wooing producers, I'd explain the advantage of bringing their show to our theatre. One big plus was that precisely because we were so small we had better union contracts that could save them $25,000-35,000 per week in running expenses. This could mean the difference between profit and loss.

I enjoyed befriending the producers who brought their shows to my theatre. They came to know that if their show ran into trouble, I would make concessions to help them out. After all, if I didn't have another show ready to come in, it would be foolish of me not to back them up. So, I might reduce the rent or the percentage of weekly gross that they had to pay us.

On some occasions, I would also give the producer a reduction in rent until another show was ready to come in, which sometimes took two to three months. As a theatre owner, you don't lose anything as long as a show is booked. You only lose if the theatre is dark.

Another rule I took to heart was to consider the show's potential for success. You don't want to book a show that appears to be a short run. You lease the theatre on an "open end" basis, which typically means that the producer cannot be asked to leave unless the show's weekly gross falls below a certain dollar amount for two consecutive weeks. Then the theatre owner can cancel the lease and ask the show to leave.

However, if I didn't have a back-up show, or if my next potential show wouldn't be ready for several months, I would let the show remain on a weekly basis and, as mentioned, help out by reducing the rent and percentage of the weekly gross. The key for a successful theatre is to stay open with a running show. Otherwise, your dark periods are very costly.

At the time, the Little Theatre charged about $10,000 in weekly rent plus 5% of gross. But if a show was struggling, we'd reduce the rent and our participation in the gross by about half. In addition, the producers of the show (the "tenant") paid the costs to operate in the theatre, which included things like wages for stage hands, ushers, and porters, plus heating, air conditioning, and lighting.

I remembered the warning I received from the Shuberts and the

Nederlanders when I first bought the theatre. They said that I couldn't be successful owning only one theatre because the show running in the house could close suddenly – since the producer is only required to give the theatre owner one week's notice. That being the case, even if I had a backup show, it might not be ready to start performances for months. My financial loss in the interim could be substantial.

Chapter 12
Gaining the Knack – for Good Fortune

As already mentioned, throughout my almost 40 years as the owner of one small theatre on Broadway, the 40 other major commercial Broadway theatres were owned and controlled by only three entities: The Shubert Organization, the Nederlander Organization and the Jujamcyn Organization. There were also three non-profit theatre companies that owned their own Broadway theatres. But these did not pose a competitive threat.

The Big Three almost never produced their own shows but they did invest in shows in order to be competitive. For instance, if a big musical that looked like it would be a hit was looking for a theatre, the three theatre owners would vie to get it into one of their venues by investing in it. On rare occasion, they might produce a show if they believed it had the potential to be highly successful.

Just as there is active competition among theatre owners to bring in a show, there is also competition between producers to find a theatre. They're hard to find because there are a lot of shows that are hits that don't vacate a theatre for years. So it's catch-as-catch-can.

For this reason, theatre owners can't really book very far in advance. They can't kick out one show to bring in another or promise a particular date to a producer unless they're doing short-term bookings. For instance, a show with a major star usually closes within four to six months because this is usually all the time the star will commit to a show. And producers usually choose to close a show rather than replace the star.

Being a single-theatre owner, whose good fortune lived or died with one show, I was in a very vulnerable position financially. The other commercial organizations could survive with several dark theatres since their running shows would support their dark houses.

Because of my situation, I had to run my theatre differently. The deals I made and my choice of shows were absolutely vital to its success. Once it was fully refurbished, the Little Theatre was considered by most to be a small, snazzy boutique competing with huge department stores. It was always a significant challenge. However, I learned to run my unique business very well.

It takes a real knack to keep a theatre lit and some people considered me to be a terrific booker because I hardly had any dark days. I attribute this success to a combination of good decisions and really good luck that lasted throughout my run as owner of the Little Theatre.

When we were really lucky, as time went on, we would have three or four shows wanting to book the theatre at the same time. So, I'd read the scripts and then make a decision based on what I thought would work the best.

Other times, however, when we had a show closing and didn't have several new ones to choose from, rather than keeping the theatre dark, I'd go ahead and book the next one that showed up – even if I didn't particularly like it and thought it wouldn't last. Then, I'd immediately start looking for another show.

In the early years, when we did have a pause between shows, that's when we continued to work on restoring the theatre. Part of my good fortune was to have my insurance business as backup in my early years on Broadway. The theatre was my first love. However, I didn't make a lot of money with it for the first years I was involved.

One of my greatest strokes of good fortune occurred when Nederlander wanted to move a show to my theatre because they had an upcoming show with Robin Williams that was already sold out. Yet, all theatres were fully booked – including theirs. It had to be a spur of the moment decision on my part. Fortunately, on this occasion, I said 'Yes,' as the show I had in our theatre was about to close.

The Robin William's show lasted four or five months – as it was a limited run. The show the Nederlanders moved to my theatre lasted almost four years. In fact, *Rock of Ages* became the longest running and most profitable show I had in nearly 40 years of running the theatre. It also came along at a very strategic time in the history of our theatre – as I will soon explain.

At one point in the show's long run Nederlander said to me, 'What a mistake I made giving you that show!' They spent half-a-million dollars moving the show to my theatre and got nothing for it.

Every day was a new adventure on Broadway. In contrast with my work in the insurance business, with its slow and steady pace, I thrived on the creativity and excitement. I also enjoyed meeting people and making deals. Once I owned my own theatre, and then won a Tony award just a few years after I'd begun producing shows, things became a whole lot more fun and very gratifying.

It would have been really easy for me to have gotten caught up in the glitz and glamour of it all. However, as Arlena will attest, I was too much of a homebody to go out hobnobbing with celebrities or to let it all go to my head.

Chapter 13
Protecting the Historic Theatre District

In the latter part of 1979, it became apparent that a real estate developer was planning to demolish three treasured theatres on 45th and 46th streets to make way for a new hotel, the Marriot Marquis. All of these theatres had incomparable acoustics and sight lines, magical intimacy, and a rich history.

One was built in 1911 and was later named for Helen Hayes. One was called the Morosco and was built in 1917. The third theatre was the Bijou, which was also built in 1917 – by the Shuberts. It was being used at the time to show art films. So, though it was lovely, the Bijou was not of any real significance to the theatre scene on Broadway. The other two theatres were.

Barbara Handman, Vice-Chair of the local Community Board, was the first outspoken critic of the plan to build a hotel – by first demolishing two beautiful old and treasured Broadway theatres. So she quietly took the issue to a variety of political and government leaders. Actors' Equity Association and its then-President, Colleen Dewhurst, simultaneously created a group called "Save the Theatres" to stop the destruction of these three beloved theatres.

Members of this group created videos, appeared on television and gave numerous interviews. Appearing on camera were such Industry luminaries as Joseph Papp, John Rubinstein, Arthur Miller, Jerry Orbach, Anne Meara, Jason Robards, Christopher Reeve, Lauren Bacall, Michael Moriarty, Adolph Green, Betty Comden, Alexander Cohen and others.

The "Save the Theatres" group staged what was probably the finest street theatre protest the city ever saw. In a last attempt to stop its destruction, a makeshift stage was set up in front of The Morosco Theatre for around-the-clock readings of Pulitzer Prize-winning plays that had been produced there.

It was not enough. On March 22, 1982, the New York City Supreme Court lifted the temporary stay of action and The Morosco Theatre was torn down. Five hundred protestors stood by crying and shouting. Two hundred people refused to leave the site and were taken away by the police.

The fight to save the theatres continued at a huge rally in front of the original Helen Hayes Theatre on 46th Street, where hundreds of Equity members gathered as the wrecking ball stood poised over the theatre. One hundred and seventy of the protestors were carted off in police vans and arrested. This protest, too, was to no avail. Among those arrested were Colleen Dewhurst, Richard Gere, Tammy Grimes, and many other well-known artists. The following month, a judge dismissed the charges against the Broadway stars that had been arrested.

Undeterred, the "Save the Theatres" group continued their fight. Although they lost the battle to save the Morosco and Helen Hayes, and did not fight to save the Bijou, they did succeed in finally getting New York City and its Landmarks Preservation Commission to designate all the remaining historic Broadway theatres – about 38 or 39 of the 41 theatres – as landmarks.

This placed additional financial burdens and use limitations on theatre owners, especially for me, as both the exterior and interior of the buildings were now subject to strict landmark regulations. These regulations are still in place today.

The regulations require that the Landmarks Commission must first approve all changes and improvements. If a theatre sustains damage, restoration is required consistent with its original structure.

One of the potential sources of significant damage are the enormous delivery trucks that drive up and down the theatre district in the middle of the night dropping off supplies for the local businesses. Since marquees often extend out to the edge of the sidewalk, a truck that makes a wide turn can inflict significant damage to it.

When this occurred to the antique marquee on a landmarked theatre, a replacement marquee would have cost the owner $20,000 to $25,000. However, the landmark designation forced the owner to replicate the old marquee, at a cost of well over $150,000. (Given that the damage was done late at night – with no witnesses – no insurance information was left behind by the truck driver to cover the costs).

The landmark designation requires that a Broadway theatre remain an operating theatre. It prevents the theatre owner from ever demolishing the theatre to build a tall office building or condominiums. Nor can owners sell their theatres to a developer who may want to do the same.

While landmark designation was a financial burden for us, my appreciation and love of theatre – and of Broadway's history, culture and unique contribution to New York City – greatly outweighed that burden and made me proud to be part of preserving the heritage and honoring the past. And down the road, as you will read, an amazing windfall appeared that more than made up for any lost opportunities.

Chapter 14
Paying Homage to a Great Lady of the Theatre

As just described, the original Helen Hayes Theatre on 46th Street – along with the Morosco and Bijou theatres – were demolished to build the Marriott Marquis Hotel despite enormous protests against it. This occurred in 1982-83, during the run of *Torch Song Trilogy* at the Little Theatre.

Our *Torch Song Trilogy* press agent, the talented and highly esteemed Betty Lee Hunt, brought the brilliant idea to me that we could now honor the iconic 'First Lady of the Theatre' – the wonderful Helen Hayes – by renaming our theatre for her. She had discussed the idea with Ken Waissman, one of our *Torch Song Trilogy* co-producers, whose prior relationship with Ms. Hayes led him to initially present the idea. I loved the idea. So, I immediately called Ms. Hayes and said to her, "Broadway cannot afford NOT to have your name on a marquee." I then went on to tell her about the Little Theatre and our desire to have it carry her name.

Ms. Hayes informed me that the she had already been approached about lending her name to the new theatre being built within the Marriot Marquis Hotel. Nonetheless, she accepted my invitation to visit us and loved our Little Theatre – especially its intimate size and superb acoustics. She recalled the numerous actors and attractions that had played there. And to our great delight, she chose us and gave us permission to rename our theatre The Helen Hayes Theatre.

Meeting Ms. Hayes during this process was an incredible thrill for me. This beautiful and extraordinary Grand Dame of the American Theatre, now in her 80s, was warm, friendly and open with me. Given where I came from, I could hardly believe that I was really there – spending time with and listening to Ms. Hayes share many theatrical stories and memories from her long career in the theatre. She reinforced my desire to succeed in finding and producing quality shows to serve the industry I loved.

On one of my birthdays many years after the theatre's renaming, a friend gifted me with a copy of the *New York Times* that was issued on the day of my actual birth, December 23, 1931. It was in a beautifully hardbound cover embossed with my name and birth date. Perusing the news and ads of that day was interesting, to say the least! However, my greatest treat was in the entertainment section's theatre listings.

Much to my surprise, I found that Helen Hayes was starring on Broadway in *The Good Fairy* (Ferenc Molnár's 1930 French comedy, English translation by Jane Hinton) produced and staged by Gilbert Miller at Henry Miller's Theatre on West 43rd Street (currently Roundabout's Stephen Sondheim Theatre).

I marveled to think that on the evening of the day I was born in Brooklyn, Helen Hayes was performing on Broadway! And fifty years later I had the privilege and pleasure of meeting her and renaming our theatre in her honor! I wish I'd had the opportunity to tell her this story as I think she would have appreciated it, too.

After we re-named the Little Theatre and put up the new marque, we held an official dedication to honor Ms. Hayes. Invitations were sent out to New York City Mayor Ed Koch and luminaries of the theatre including Joe Papp, Colleen Dewhurst, Ellen Burstyn, Joshua Logan and Ellis Rabb – all of whom came to pay their glowing respects to the incomparable Ms. Hayes.

When it was Ms. Hayes' turn to address the gathering, she spoke of her love of theatre, her many years as a performer, and the thrill of having her name once again lighting up Broadway. Her words lit up my heart. It was a delight to pay homage to this beautiful artist and to have her name adorn our theatre marquee.

PLAYBILL

THE HELEN HAYES THEATRE

Martin Markinson and Donald Tick
invite you to join them
and

HELEN HAYES

when
The Little Theatre
will be renamed
in honor of
The First Lady
of the
American Stage.

The ceremony will take place
on July 21, 1983
at 11:00 A.M. at

240 West 44th Street
New York, New York 10036

The Helen Hayes Theatre

Invitation to the Dedication and Renaming of the Theatre

Alex Cohen, Colleen Dewhurst, Joseph Papp, Martin
Markinson, Ellen Burstyn, Mayor Edward Koch,
Helen Hayes, Joshua Logan, Ellis Rabb

The dedication of

THE HELEN HAYES THEATRE

Thursday

July 21, 1983

at 11 A.M.

240 West 44th Street

New York, New York

HONORED GUESTS

The Honorable

Edward I. Koch

Mayor of the City of New York

and

Ellen Burstyn

Alexander H. Cohen

Colleen Dewhurst

Martin Markinson

Joshua Logan

Joseph Papp

Ellis Rabb

Donald Tick

Program listing Honored Guests

Alex Cohen, Ellen Burstyn, Colleen Dewhurst,
Helen Hayes and Martin Markinson

Helen Hayes in front of the Helen Hayes Theatre

Helen Hayes visiting the theatre to meet
the stars of *Torch Song Trilogy.*
Martin Markinson, Court Miller and
Harvey Fierstein with Ms. Hayes

Chapter 15
Increasing Our
Seating Capacity

Following the re-naming ceremony, we continued renovating and rebuilding with renewed vigor until we had the beautiful gem of a theatre it is today. But there was still more to do.

One evening I went to see a show at a Shubert Theatre. Sitting in the first row, my knees practically touching the stage, the thought occurred to me that the Helen Hayes actually had more room than we thought. I realized that we could install two more rows of seats without people's knees brushing against the stage.

The HHT was a union-designated 500-seat capacity "Middle House" with attendant favorable "Middle House" union rates and rules. And Broadway is most definitely a unionized industry. It always has been. Most Broadway theatres run subject to about 14 different collective agreements, each requiring negotiations

Being a member of The Broadway League – which covers theatres in New York and many other U.S. cities – our theatre was signatory to the collective agreements negotiated by the League on behalf of the Broadway theatre owners. This made it politically difficult and almost impossible for me to do any of my own negotiating with the various unions in the 1980s and early 1990s; for the Broadway League negotiated on behalf of all of its members. Fortunately, my small theatre was subject to only about seven of the fourteen agreements at the time.

The quandary I faced was that I needed 100 more seats to financially compete in the escalating Broadway economics. But then I would exceed the 500-seat "Middle House" limit with its attendant union breaks. My solution was to define my own parameters and negotiate my own union deals, a decision that forced me to leave the League.

This meant that I couldn't vote in the Tony's anymore or get my free Tony tickets. But it was more important to me to do my own negotiations.

I presented my special case as still the smallest theatre on Broadway and sought agreement to continue working with the union at more appropriate and favorable rates and rules with 600 seats. My appeal worked. I successfully installed the extra seats; and I also operated with better union contracts than the larger theatres. Eventually the League let me become a member again, while also allowing me to continue to do my own negotiating.

With 600 seats and decent union contracts, the HHT was able to attract better shows that garnered Tony nominations and awards. I didn't raise the rent with the extra 100 seats but let the producers enjoy a higher weekly potential for profit. So as long as I did well and was happy about it, I never squeezed for more. That was not my nature.

Chapter 16
Torch Song Trilogy – Our Great Theatrical Triumph

I am often asked to name the production of which I am most proud. There is no contest. I talked about the thrill of winning my first Tony Award with *Torch Song Trilogy* in the Foreword to this book. Now I want to go back and explain in more detail how it all came to be.

I had heard favorable things about the off-Broadway version of this show, written and performed as three separate one-act plays by Harvey Fierstein and produced by The Glines (John Glines and Larry Lane). The plays were called, *International Stud, Fugue in a Nursery,* and *Widows and Children First.* Together, they told the story of a Jewish homosexual drag queen torch singer named Arnold Beckoff, who was living in New York City in the late '70s and early 80's.

While I was initially resistant to the theme, my then-attorney, Susan Myerberg (who later became my theatre manager and general counsel), insisted that I go see the play. Curious enough to see the first show, I was so impressed, that I went back to see the second and third.

The stories of *Torch Song Trilogy* haunted me. I had never really thought about what life was like for a gay person growing up in a straight world. Fierstein's plays acquainted me with some of the issues they faced.

Seeing these shows, I realized that homosexuals only want every bit as much love, respect and happiness as anyone else. So I definitely wanted to bring the play to Broadway and specifically to my own theatre to present these issues to a mainstream Broadway audience.

The creators and the original producers all agreed with me that it would work even better if all three plays were brought together into one. However, the combined shows would then run for four hours.

Again, everyone outside of our *Torch Song* circle said I was 'nuts' – that it could never be done. "What the hell are you thinking?" I was asked more than once. "A gay-themed show? There's never been one like this on Broadway – and it will be too long. It's crazy, risky."

Rather than heed these warnings I decided to go with my gut and take the risk. *Torch Song Trilogy* was not only a wonderful story, I felt it was also a very important one to bring to a wide audience for reasons I'll explain shortly. So, I joined the producing team and determined to bring it to the Little Theatre.

We asked Fierstein to cut it down to three-and-a-half hours. It was three acts with two intermissions, so we also cut intermission times. Because I was so afraid of bad reviews, there was no "Opening Night." It was simply deemed a transfer from off-Broadway to Broadway.

Like life, the show was a process. For the first six months, it attracted primarily gay audiences. My partner, Donald Tick, and I put in our own money to keep it running. As the theatre owners, we were able to reduce the rent for the same reason.

After six or seven months, the word-of-mouth was so good that we started attracting the heterosexual community as well. Suddenly, we were making a real profit. The show caught on and ran for three years, which was unheard of for a play like this.

I then found out that I was right, and I felt very proud of that. The show was indeed a very important one. It offered heterosexuals the chance to see life in the homosexual world, where they discovered gay/lesbian people desire the same quality of life that everyone else does.

Many people believe that this groundbreaking play, by entering the mainstream via Broadway, provided an opening for gay people to come into their own with personal freedom and pride. It also inspired other producers of movies, TV and Broadway shows to take the leap and present gay-themed stories with gay actors. All of us involved in this unexpected hit show felt deeply gratified by the waves of positive change it initiated!

Although we began the Broadway performances of the *Torch Song Trilogy* in June 1982, Tony eligibility deadlines meant the show was not eligible to be considered for an award until June 1983 – a full year later.

I described in the Foreword that life-changing moment when I was called up to accept the Tony for the best play of the year. Not only was that evening one of the great highlights of my life, it also started me seriously thinking that perhaps it was time to change careers. For after that night I became noticed in the industry as a producer and also as a major theatre owner by virtue of having booked into my theatre a Tony-award winning show.

As Carol Lawson reported in the New York Times the following day, June 6, 1983:

> "*Torch Song Trilogy*" ... tells the story of Arnold Beckoff, a nice Jewish boy of "great wit and want" ... a homosexual and transvestite who makes his living ... on stage.

> "Everybody was so scared that I was going to say something embarrassing to all of you," said the smiling Mr. Fierstein, who had a tough time getting his play produced. It originated in 1978 as ... one-act plays at ... La Mama Theatre and was ... presented as a trilogy Off Broadway. When it moved to Broadway ..., few people predicted ... the play would last long with uptown audiences.

"Torch Song Trilogy" won [the Tony Award for Best
Play] over ... two dramas that were thought to be
the leading contenders ... – Plenty, ... by ... David
Hare, and 'Night, Mother,' Marsha Norman's Pulitzer
Prize-winning drama ...

I still chuckle when I remember watching two elderly ladies standing outside the theatre (after we'd changed the name), discussing
whether or not to go in and see *Torch Song*. One said, "I hear it's about
homosexuals. That doesn't appeal to me." Her friend looked up at the
marquee. "Well, how bad can it be if Helen Hayes is playing in it?"
They went inside.

Torch Song Trilogy went on to play in London and elsewhere.
Harvey also starred in the popular movie based on his play, along
with Matthew Broderick and Anne Bancroft.

Coincidentally, when *Torch Song* was still off-off Broadway, the
young, unknown actor Matthew Broderick played the son. When
Neil Simon went to see the show, he chose Broderick to star in *Brighton
Beach Memoirs*, a show Simon was doing on Broadway. That put the actor on the road to fame. It also won him a Tony for Best Performance
by a Featured Actor in a Play at the same Tony Awards ceremony
where *Torch Song Trilogy* and Harvey Fierstein won for Best Play and
Best Actor! Harvey later went on to win other Tony Awards for his
writing and acting and was inducted into the American Theatre Hall
of Fame in 2007.

HARVEY FIERSTEIN'S

TORCH SONG TRILOGY

KENNETH WAISSMAN   MARTIN MARKINSON
JOHN GLINES   LAWRENCE LANE
with DelMar and Donald Tick

present

The Glines Production of

HARVEY FIERSTEIN'S

TORCH SONG TRILOGY

Stage Design by   Costume Design by   Lighting Design by
BILL STABILE   MARDI PHILIPS   SCOTT PINKNEY

Musical Direction & Arrangements for   Original Music for
International Stud   Fugue in a Nursery
NED LEVY   ADA JANIK

General Management   Press Representative
Theatre Now, Inc.   Hunt-Pucci Associates

Production Stage Manager   Associate Producer
Herb Vogler   Howard Perloff

Directed by

PETER POPE

THE LITTLE THEATRE
44th Street West of Broadway

Chapter 17
Taking a Larger Leap of Faith – Into the World of Theatre

In mid-1989, Donald Tick, my partner in both the insurance business and our Broadway Theatre, approached me with a serious issue. It was clear to him that most of my time, energy and interest was in the theatre. And while I did not neglect any of my responsibilities in our insurance business, it felt to him that he was carrying the greater weight of responsibility for our company's success.

We had many conversations on the subject and I understood and agreed with Donald's assessment. Clearly, it was time for me to decide whether to remain in the insurance business or to break up our partnership in it.

There was really no disputing where my passions lay. But it was still not an easy decision. I'd been relying on income from the insurance business to support my family and pay our mortgage. Whatever money we were making through the rental of our theatre, we were immediately reinvesting in renovations to turn it into a truly beautiful, warm and inviting venue.

Nevertheless, the time had arrived for me to choose between necessity and passion. I once again went with my gut feeling and, regardless of my financial concerns, sold my interest in the insurance business to Donald.

I supported my family with the income from the buy-out until the theatre became truly profitable. Now I was 100% involved as a theatre owner/producer, and was absolutely determined to succeed. I was finally able to fully engage in the business I loved.

Chapter 18
'Let's Do Lunch!' – Dining with the Stars on Broadway

Sardi's is the restaurant where it all comes together on Broadway: Great food, great fun and some great business deals. Located right next door to the Helen Hayes Theatre on 44th Street between Broadway and 8th Avenue, it has been an integral part of the Broadway scene for three generations. In fact, it is among the most popular restaurants in the whole theatre district.

Many important theatrical decisions have been made over lunch at Sardi's and many opening night parties have been held there. Members of the general public enjoy going to Sardi's in hopes of seeing celebrities who dine there before and after the theatre.

Among the many things that Sardi's is known for are the caricatures of Broadway celebrities including actors, directors and producers. As a theatre owner and producer, as well as a next-door neighbor, Sardi's contacted me once I'd become well known asking to make a caricature of me. When I agreed, they sent me to be photographed and then sent the photo to a caricature artist. Once my image was hanging on the wall, every time our grandchildren were in New York they'd go to Sardi's for lunch and point out my picture to their friends. "Hey, that's my Poppi; that's my grandfather."

Because Arlena and I lived most of the time in Santa Fe, New Mexico, I only came to New York about six times a year for a week to 10 days, during which time I'd see eight or nine shows. That way, I'd end up seeing about 40 shows each year. Of course, I always attended opening night at my own theatre.

On one occasion when I was in town and was going to attend a Wednesday matinee, I decided to have lunch at Sardi's first. The waiter happened to sit me at a table directly under my caricature. Next to me was a table with four women. They were obviously from out-of-town and I couldn't help but overhear their conversation. They were trying to identify as many of the caricatures hanging on the wall as they could.

I noticed them looking at me and whispering to each other. One of them then turned to me and said, "Excuse me, is that a picture of you?" After replying, "Yes," they asked who are the other people on the wall with you? "They are mostly theatrical producers, as I am," I answered.

"Oh my God! I've never met a Broadway producer before," one of them said. "How long do they keep your picture on the wall?" I explained, "If you have two flops in a row, they move you to the second floor. If you have another they move you to the third floor. If you don't have a hit show for three years they hang you in the men's bathroom." The ladies were delighted with my spontaneous response.

With special thanks to and kind permission from Sardi's (V. Max Klimavicius, President), two photos from Sardi's follow this chapter.

The Polish Tea Room – otherwise known as the Café Edison – was thusly dubbed by theatre impresario Manny Azenberg in honor of its Polish owners and founders, two holocaust survivors, Frances and Harry Edelstein, known to all of us simply as Frances and Harry. This little restaurant in the Hotel Edison on W 47th Street was quite the opposite of the famed and lavish Russian Tea Room. The 'Polish' served an inexpensive and delicious fare of Eastern European home style cooking that was popular with many people in the theatre business – including producers, directors, actors and playwrights. Alas, the Polish closed in 2014 and is merely a fond memory now.

I was having lunch there one day and sitting at the table next to me were two young actresses who apparently just came from an audition. I overheard them discussing their experiences. One of them said, "This was my third call back. The director was so nasty and difficult with me." The other actress sitting with her quickly responded, "Fuck Him!" The first immediately replied, "I did! And I still didn't get the part." Obviously, this was many years before the #MeToo movement, when the 'casting couch' was seen as an unavoidable hurdle to a successful career by many aspiring young actresses.

One day in 1983 I was having lunch at Sardi's with Wayne Adams a producer friend who had just gotten back from Chicago where he'd seen a show that he thought had potential for Broadway. He suggested I go see it. I asked him what theatre it was playing at, and he told me that it wasn't really at an actual theatre. It was in the basement of the Highland Park Church in Chicago. Since he was impressed with the play, and I admired his theatrical taste, I decided to go.

Staged by a group called the Steppenwolf Theatre Company – founded in 1974 by Gary Sinise, Terry Kinney and Jeff Perry – the show was called *And a Nightingale Sang* by C. P. Taylor. Once I saw it I agreed with Wayne that it was a wonderful story with an impressive cast and production. We decided to produce it together and bring it directly to Broadway.

This was in 1983 while *Torch Song Trilogy* was running at The Helen Hayes. So, we had to find a New York theatre where we could just lift *Nightingale* as is, with the same cast and sets.

I heard that Alex Cohen, one of the more prominent producers at the time, had just booked the Vivian Beaumont Theatre at Lincoln Center for a new show he was doing. Also located at Lincoln Center was a smaller theatre called The Mitzi Newhouse, which had not been used in several years. It was perfect for our show. The Lincoln

Center agreed so we now had a theatre and opened the show to very warm reviews.

The star of *Nightingale* was Joan Allen, who was one of the actors from the Steppenwolf group. Some of the others were Gary Sinise, John Malkovich, John Mahony, and Terry Kinney. When I met them in Chicago, they all worked at jobs during the day and performed in the evenings. Needless to say, after being introduced to New York they went on to become major Broadway actors and movie stars. Today, the Steppenwolf Group not only has its own theatre in Chicago, they also have become a major producer of shows, several of which have come to Broadway.

The Friar's Club – serves a delicious Saturday brunch that I make an effort to frequent whenever I am in New York. This is a club whose membership consists mostly of celebrities in the entertainment industry. I would see many of the old-time comedians there when they were in town, such as Jerry Lewis, Norm Crosby, Buddy Hackett and Henny Youngman to name just a few. It was the best entertainment around, as they used to joke to one another while sitting at different tables eating their meals.

One Saturday, I was at a table next to Henny Youngman and overheard him and his friends discussing children and childbirth. Henny announced, "I was so ugly when I was born, the doctor slapped my mother." Shortly after that, Buddy Hackett shouted from his table to Henny that he had just come from a funeral at Riverside Chapel and saw a large picture of him in the lobby. Youngman asked, "What was my picture doing there?" Hackett replied, "There was a sign over it saying, "Coming Attractions." I still get a chuckle remembering them.

That leads me to another fond memory. When I was a very young man, I had no one around to teach me good manners, proper dress, how to carry myself and relate to other people. So, as previously mentioned, I chose as my model Cary Grant, the most popular movie star of his day. And I went to see every one of his movies, sometimes several times.

I had long admired Grant's general style, manner of speaking, and graceful movements so began learning by watching him. He was more or less my mentor in this regard.

Each year, The Friar's Club honored a celebrity with a black tie affair at the Waldorf Astoria in New York. One year, they were honoring Cary Grant. There was absolutely no way I was going to miss that ceremony! So, there I was in my black tie, watching him being honored.

At intermission, I went to the men's room. In those days, they had the big, long urinals. As I was relieving myself, I glanced to my left. And there, peeing alongside me, was Cary Grant. I was absolutely stunned, and kept turning, little by little to my left, to get a better look. I suddenly realized that one more turn and I would be peeing on his leg! After that experience, when anyone would ask me which celebrities I knew best, I would simply say, "Cary Grant and I peed together at the Waldorf Astoria."

Caricatures at Sardi's - Martin Markinson's
is top row, second from left.

and a Nightingale Sang...

Produced by WAYNE ADAMS, SHERWIN M. GOLDMAN, MARTIN MARKINSON in association with WESTPORT PRODUCTIONS, William Twohill Executive Producer Written by C.P. TAYLOR Scenery by DAVID JENKINS Costumes by JESS GOLDSTEIN Lighting by KEVIN RIGDON Sound by DAVID BUDRIES Production Stage Manager DOROTHY J. MAFFEI Featuring JOAN ALLEN, JOHN CARPENTER, ROBERT CORNTHWAITE, PETER FRIEDMAN, FRANCIS GUINAN, MOIRA HARRIS and BEVERLY MAY Directed by TERRY KINNEY

MITZI E. NEWHOUSE THEATER AT LINCOLN CENTER
in the Vivian Beaumont Theater Building, 150 West 65th Street

Chapter 19
Shows That Played at the Helen Hayes Theatre 1985 - 2015

With great appreciation to and generous permission from *Playbill*, I quote from their archives to list the shows that played at our theatre following *Torch Song Trilogy*. (© Playbill, Inc. New York City. All rights reserved. Philip Birsh, President & CEO, Playbill, Inc. New York City)

 Torch Song was followed by such varied productions as *The News* (1985), a rock musical about sensational journalism; *Corpse!* (1985), a comedy thriller starring Keith Baxter and Milo O'Shea; *Oh Coward!* (1986), a revival of Roderick Cook's 1972 revue of Noel Coward songs and skits, starring Cook, Patrick Quinn, and Catherine Cox; *Mummenschanz/The New Show* (1986), a new edition of the popular mime show; *The Nerd* (1987), Larry Shue's amusing comedy about a man posing as a jerk to help out a friend; Scott Bakula and Alison Fraser in *Romance/Romance* (1988), two charming one-act musicals that moved here from off-Broadway; Mandy Patinkin in *Concert: Dress*

Casual (1989), the singing actor in a diverting program; *Artist Descending a Staircase* (1989), Tom Stoppard's complex comedy about the art world; and *Miss Margarida's Way* (1990), Estelle Parsons in a return engagement of the acclaimed one-woman show about an explosive teacher and her unruly pupils.

Prelude to a Kiss (1990), Craig Lucas's fantasy that originally starred Alec Baldwin off-Broadway, moved here with Timothy Hutton in Baldwin's role, plus Mary-Louise Parker, Barnard Hughes, and Debra Monk. The 1990's also saw *The High Rollers Social and Pleasure Club* (1992), a musical revue set in New Orleans; *3 From Brooklyn* (1992), Roslyn Kind in a revue about Brooklyn; *Shakespeare for my Father* (1993), Lynn Redgrave in a highly praised one-woman show about her late father, actor Michael Redgrave; and Joan Rivers in *Sally Marr ... and her Escorts* (1994). Rivers not only starred in this play about Lenny Bruce's mother, but also wrote it with Ernie Sanders and Lonny Price. She was nominated for a Tony Award for her performance. The voice of young Lenny Bruce was supplied by Jason Woliner.

In November 1994, the popular Flying Karamazov Brothers juggling troupe opened here in their fourth Broadway performance. They called their vaudeville show *The Flying Karamazov Brothers: Do the Impossible*. They entertained for 50 performances.

The theatre's next tenant was *Defending the Caveman*, a comic monologue about the differences between men and women. It had a prosperous run of 671 performances, a record for a non-musical solo show.

Caveman made way for another success: Alfred Uhry's *The Last Night of Ballyhoo* (1997), starring Paul Rudd and Dana Ivey, which ran for 557 performances. The play dealt with the conflicts within an Atlanta Jewish family at the time of the 1939 premiere of the film, "Gone with the Wind" in that city. The play won the Tony Award as Best Play of the season, making Uhry the only playwright at that time to win a Tony Award, a Pulitzer Prize (for *Driving Miss Daisy*), and an Academy Award (for the screenplay of *Driving Miss Daisy*).

This theatre's next two entries were not successful; *Getting and Spending* (1998) was a play by Michael J. Chepiga. And *Band in Berlin* was a musical about the Comedian Harmonists, a real-life troupe of singers popular in Germany in the 1920s but banned by Hitler in the 1930s because the troupe included Jewish and non-Jewish performers.

In 1999, *Night Must Fall,* a revival of Emlyn Williams' 1936 thriller about a psychotic killer, moved to the Hayes from the Lyceum Theatre. Based on an actual murder case, it starred Matthew Broderick, Judy Parfitt, and Pamela J. Gray. It was produced by Tony Randall's National Arts Theatre, and ran for 96 performances.

Night Must Fall was followed by a comedy called *Epic Proportions* by Larry Coen and David Crane. It spoofed the absurdities of filming a Hollywood biblical spectacle with thousands of extras—all played by a cast of just eight. It starred Kristin Chenoweth, Alan Tudyk, Jeremy Davidson and Richard B. Shull. Unfortunately, Shull died during the play's run. He was replaced by Lewis J. Stadlen. The play ran for 84 performances.

On May 1, 2000, *Dirty Blonde,* a hit off-Broadway, moved to our theatre from the New York Theatre Workshop. The comedy dealt with the famed actress/playwright, Mae West. It was written by Claudia Shear, who also starred in a dual role as West and one of her fans. The play was conceived by Shear and James Lapine, who directed it. Kevin Chamberlin and Bob Stillman co-starred in a variety of roles. The play proved an instant hit and was nominated for five Tony Awards.

Hershey Felder wrote, acted in, and played piano in *George Gershwin Alone,* his solo tribute to the great Broadway composer. It opened April 30, 2001 and shared its "fascinatin' rhythm" with audiences. It has gone on with great success to play around the world.

Composer Andrew Lloyd Webber and prolific British playwright, Alan Ayckbourn, shared an interest in P.G. Wodehouse's stories about dim-witted aristocrat Bernie Wooster and his super-humanly capable butler, Jeeves. In the 1970s, between Lloyd Webber's hits, *Jesus Christ Superstar* and *Evita,* they collaborated on a flop musical adaptation called *Jeeves.*

In the late 1990s the two writers returned to this project, determined to whack it into shape. The result was *By Jeeves,* a scaled-down version of the story (including the lovely takeout song, "Half a Moment"), which had a modest run in London. The show moved to the Hayes on October 28, 2001, just weeks after the September 11 terrorist attacks downtown. Lloyd Webber himself attended the box office opening day, greeting ticket buyers on the sidewalk out front and congratulating New Yorkers on their stiff upper lip. The generous gesture didn't help the slightly tweaked and very British musical, which lasted only 73 performances, the composer's shortest Broadway run to date.

Michele Low's black-comedy, wish-fulfillment play, *The Smell of the Kill*, featured a group of women who are so sick of their loutish husbands that they concoct a plan to murder then all. The play opened March 26, 2002, and closed after 40 performances.

Writer Rupert Holmes, better known as a composer, lyricist and mystery writer for shows such as *The Mystery of Edwin Drood*, earned a Tony nomination for his gentle solo show, *Say Goodnight, Gracie*, a portrait of the great comedian, George Burns. Frank Gorshin embodied Burns for 396 performances, starting October 10, 2002.

Gracie was followed by another Tony-nominated show, William Gibson's *Golda's Balcony*, in which Tova Feldshuh played Israel's founding mother, Golda Meir. Feldshuh was also Tony-nominated as Best Actress in a Play, and incarnated the Prime Minister for 493 performances, from October 15, 2003, to January 2, 2005.

Jackie Mason returned to Broadway with his eighth comedy show, this one titled *Jackie Mason: Freshly Squeezed*. It was filled with his patented takes on politics, culture and the modern world and stayed at the Hayes for 172 performances.

Cheech Marin, half of the comedy team of Cheech and Chong, made his Broadway directorial debut with *Latinologues*, a showcase for Latino comedians. The bill featured Rick Najera, Rene Lavan, and Shirley A. Rumierk. It played 93 performances starting October 13, 2005.

Sarah Jones, daughter of a United Nations diplomat, put her observations to work in *Bridge & Tunnel*, a solo show in which she embodied a whole rainbow of recent immigrants to New York. It opened January 26, 2006, and occupied the Hayes for 213 performances, winning the 2006 Tony Award for Best Special Theatrical Event.

The popular downtown comedy musical club act known as "Kiki and Herb" came uptown to the Hayes for a 27-performance, late-summer 2006 limited run titled *Kiki & Herb: Alive on Broadway*.

From this semi-drag act, the Hayes next turned itself over to a puppet show – albeit a distinguished one. *Jay Johnson: The Two and Only* (September 2006) was also an autobiography. In addition to traditional puppet high jinks, Johnson and his puppet "co-star," Bob, narrated Johnson's life story as a ventriloquist, most notably his relationship with his mentor. Though the show had a limited run of only two months and was gone before the June Tony Awards, it won the 2007 Tony for Best Theatrical Event.

On July 10, 2007, the Hayes got one of the great sleeper hits of modern times, a full-scale musical called *Xanadu*. It was based on a spectacular flop disco-era film musical of the same name, but re-conceived as a tongue-in-cheek camp-fest by librettist Douglas Carter Beane and directed by Chris Ashley. Cheyenne Jackson (replacing James Carpinello, who injured himself during previews) played a man whose life dream is to open a roller disco. Kerry Butler played one of the Greek muses who decided to help him. Mary Testa and Jackie Hoffman played her sister muses who plot her failure. It also featured Tony Roberts as Zeus. The musical fantasy drew incredulous reviews from critics who couldn't believe how much they liked it, and *Xanadu* roller-skated its way to a 512-performance run.

Following *Xanadu*, "New Vaudeville" clown Slava Polunin transferred his *Slava's Snowshow* to the Hayes in December 2008, after more than 1,000 performances Off-Broadway. It played out the holidays then prepared to tour.

In January 2009, the Hayes became the third Broadway stop for the long-running hit, *The 39 Steps*, which had opened at the American Airlines Theatre, then moved to the Cort Theatre for several months. In early 2010, *The 39 Steps* took its fourth New York step and moved Off-Broadway.

In its place came *Next Fall*, Geoffrey Nauffts' play about religion and gay relationships, which had been developed by the Naked Angel's Company off-Broadway. It lasted for 132 performances.

Comedian Colin Quinn, best known for his stint on "Saturday Night Live," returned to the Hayes – having performed his *Irish Wake* here in 1998 – with his new one-man show, *Colin Quinn: Long Story Short*, on November 9, 2010. The show, directed by Jerry Seinfeld, ran for 135 performances and was filmed for television by HBO.

Our final show before the 2015 sale to Second Stage Theatre was the enormous surprise hit *Rock of Ages*, which began performances in March 2011 and broke HHT house records, week after week.

Rock of Ages, a rock/jukebox musical with a book by Chris D'Arienzo and classic 1980s glam/hair metal rock, was directed by Kristin Hanggi and choreographed by Kelly Devine. Ethan Popp was music supervisor, arranger and orchestrator. This hilarious, joyous show moved to the HHT from a larger Broadway theatre where it opened with Constantine Maroulis of American Idol fame, who also closed the historic almost 4+ year run at the HHT.

The show was a surprise success for Broadway and also for me. It brought a younger and less traditional crowd to Broadway and received five Tony nominations.

As I previously shared, before it came to the HHT, *Rock of Ages* wasn't filling the larger Nederlander theatre in which it played. At the Hayes, however, because our union rates reduced the weekly expense of running the show by $25-35,000 per week, the production was able to do extraordinarily well. It ran for 2,328 performances, closing on January 18, 2015 as the 29th-longest running show in Broadway history.

Rock of Ages toured across the US and worldwide including Japan, Australia, and the United Kingdom. There was also a resident production on cruise ships. The 2012 movie starred Tom Cruise, Alec Baldwin, Mary J. Blige, Julianne Hough and Paul Giamatti.

The Helen Hayes Theatre remained Broadway's smallest theatre and was fiercely independent in both its management and programming. *Rock of Ages, Torch Song Trilogy,* and *Gemini* are in the top 70s of Longest Running Shows on Broadway.

Part II
The Big Business of
Show Business

Chapter 20
The Adventure Goes On –
With a Little Side Career

Back in New Mexico, the Director of Theatre Arts at the College of Santa Fe learned about my work on Broadway. So, he contacted me to ask if I would make a presentation to the graduating theatre majors about what it takes to produce a show on Broadway – along with other aspects of the theatre business. I happily agreed to do so and continued for the next 10 years.

The 20-25 students in each of the classes I addressed had diverse career goals, some wanting to be set designers and others aspiring to be actors, directors, or producers. Twice a year I would speak to the classes extemporaneously about my experiences on Broadway as a theatre owner and a producer of plays and musicals.

The students were hearing things first hand that their classes were not equipped to teach them. Thus, they were fascinated and full of questions. Our sessions together usually lasted about 90 minutes – including my presentation followed by Q&A's. After some of my talks I would pass around my Tony Award and watch how alive they became when examining it.

I lectured twice a semester and spoke to theatre students, faculty and alumni at several colleges across the country, including Skidmore and Yale. I became very passionate about sharing my knowledge and inspiring young people. And I so appreciated the responses I received from both the students and the adults that attended my talks. I was speaking from a world few had ever experienced up close. And I found their enjoyment of what I shared very gratifying.

During this period of time, on April 27, 2006, Donald Tick, my dear friend and close business partner for over 40 years – the co-owner with me of the Helen Hayes Theatre – passed away. This was a very sad day for me as well, of course, for his entire family and all of his friends. I still miss Donald and our wonderful friendship. His name continued to appear as a principal of the Little Theatre Group. His oldest son, Jeffrey Tick, then joined me in handling the Helen Hayes Theatre's daily operations.

Chapter 21
Dealing With Controversy

In a recent talk I gave to theatre students, one of the questions asked was, "In all of your years producing shows and operating your theatre, did you encounter many controversies?"

In recalling my experiences with actors, directors, authors, agents and many union negotiations, I felt very fortunate to not have been involved in any major confrontations. I got along well with people in general. My attitude was to find out what they needed or wanted and try to make it work for them if I possibly could.

For instance, in 1982, when Faye Dunaway was starring in a show at the Hayes, she did not like the color of the dressing rooms or the lounge area. So we repainted them for her.

When Joan Rivers performed at the Hayes she wanted all of her exercise equipment brought to the theatre. Since we had 11 dressing rooms and only three other actors in the show, we said, 'Yes," of course.

The one difficult controversy I remember was when I brought a show from London to the Helen Hayes. It was a murder mystery called *Corpse,* by Gerald Moon. It was a hit in London and starred the popular English actor Keith Baxter, who was unknown in the States. I brought him to Broadway since he was the star in London and had been with the show since the beginning.

When we were about to start rehearsals in New York we hired a well-known theatre actor, Milo O'Shea, to play the second lead. Milo was a respected and popular performer. So when we hung the marquee announcing the show, we put his name as top billing above Keith's. Our reasoning was that a recognized Broadway actor could create more ticket sales. That's where I made my mistake.

Before we started rehearsals, Keith Baxter saw the marquee with Milo's name above his and then I heard from his agent. "No way is that acceptable," he told me. "Keith made this a hit in London and agreed to come to Broadway with the show. We can't start rehearsals until this is corrected."

Thinking that I had the wisdom of King Solomon, I proposed to have the marquee display both their names side-by-side. I thought that before I spend another $10,000 on a new marquee (which is what it would cost to design and install it), it would be wise to check with the agent.

"That won't work either," he advised me. "Keith's name must appear as top billing or we don't go into rehearsals." Fortunately Milo O'Shea was very understanding and said, "It was Keith's show in London, he came over here with it and he should have top billing." So it was settled!

There can be many controversies when producing shows. However, I've never allowed disagreements to escalate. I resolved them quickly. Not being involved in any major disputes made my theatrical career very satisfying.

Another place where controversies often occur is between union members on one side and theatre owners and producers on the other because of conflicting interests when negotiating labor contracts. However, here, too, I sought ways to create equitable solutions that worked for everyone.

So when I was asked to give presentations to members of the local One Union in New York City, to help the membership better understand how difficult it is to put a whole show together, I was delighted to do so. I believe this further strengthened our sense of connection and of working together toward common objectives.

Typically, on Broadway, there are crews assigned to every theatre. If a theatre is dark, however, stagehands and technicians are free to accept work in other theatres. Once their own theatre books a show, however, they leave where they've been working and return 'home.' I deeply appreciated the degree of loyalty and support that I received from all the people who worked at our theatre.

Martin Markinson, Gary Leaverton and Robert Fox
present

KEITH BAXTER
MILO O'SHEA in

C O R P S E !

A Comedy Thriller by
GERALD MOON

with
SCOTT LaFEBER
and
PAULINE FLANAGAN

Settings by
ALAN TAGG
Costumes by
LOWELL DETWEILER
Lighting by
RICHARD WINKLER

Directed by
JOHN TILLINGER

HELEN HAYES THEATRE
—240 West 44th Street—

Chapter 22
FAQ's – Answers to Some Frequently Asked Questions

Given that I shared my knowledge and experiences on Broadway with many people over the years, I decided to answer some of the most frequently asked questions here.

"Exactly what and where is Broadway?" When people say they're going to New York City to see some shows on Broadway, many of them don't know exactly what that means, where it is or what it represents.

Here's what I explain: Broadway is a street in Manhattan but all the theatres and shows are not on that one street. Broadway is a specifically defined district that runs from 41st to 54th Street, between Sixth and Eight Avenues.

Lincoln Center and Times Square are also included.

Any theatre in that area that has at least 500 seats is considered a Broadway house and is subject to theatrical union jurisdiction.

Any theatre outside of that area, regardless of its size, is considered off-Broadway and is therefore less prestigious.

There are 41 theatres in the Broadway District, all of which are eligible for the Tony Awards. Other than several non-profit theatres (Lincoln Center, Roundabout Theatre Company, Manhattan Theatre Club, Circle in the Square and, most recently, Second Stage Theatre), the balance are owned by only four organizations, the Shuberts, the Nederlanders, Jujamcyn – and by myself with the Tick Family from 1979-2015.

The season typically runs from June to June, and the just-completed season is celebrated at the Tony Awards, which is held sometime in June.

What qualities make a show a classic? When a show is first produced on Broadway and becomes a big hit that earns a large profit, it's considered a classic. However, this does not mean that if you do a revival of it – that it will automatically be a hit.

Do shows run nightly? Most shows have eight performances a week – Tuesday through Sunday with Matinees on Wednesday and Saturday.

What are the typical lengths for the run of a show? You could close a show the first night, week or month – or it could last for 20 years, as *Phantom* has. There is no way of knowing how long a show can run. It depends very much on how well it does at the box office.

What are the costs of producing a show? The cost for producing a play in 2015 was about $3,000,000. A sizeable musical costs somewhere between $8,000,000 – 18,000,000 because of the lavish sets, costumes, the size of orchestra, cast and crew needed to run the show.

How much money can investors make? In the papers that attorneys draw up for investors, they make it clear that investing in theatre is a very risky business. In most cases, you may not make a profit and you may lose your entire investment. So, investors have to be people of means who can afford to lose.

In my experience, perhaps two out of five shows are successful monetarily. So, if you invested in all five shows, you likely lost money on three and maybe made it back on the other two. That's why producers do not try to entice investors. We may be enthusiastic about the potential for success of a particular show. But we let investors know the risks.

A flop and a hit are not measured by how long a show runs but by whether you make any money and pay back the investors. If you pay back the investors and close right after, then the show is considered a success. If investors don't get paid back, then the show is considered a flop no matter how long it runs.

On the other hand, when a show does really well, the returns can be enormous. I'm told that if you invested $1000 in *Fiddler on the Roof*, your return would have been $100,000. People who invested in *Hamilton* will get quite a lot back; Phantom is reaching its 30th year; and Chicago has been running for 15 years. The returns for investors on big hits like these become like an annuity.

What role do critics play? Critics used to have a lot more influence than they do today. When the leading 20th Century producer David Merrick was still working, there were seven newspapers – each of which had a theatre critic.

Today, there are only *The NY Times, New York Post,* and *New York Daily News* – with the *Times* being the most influential. Years ago, if you received a good review in the *Times,* then you knew you had a hit and you would have a line at the box office all the next day.

Now, even if the *Times* gives an excellent review, the show may not succeed. Conversely, a show with a star might not be affected at all by a bad review. The theatre will still be packed. So, the critic doesn't matter nearly as much as in the past.

There are also additional sources for reviews these days – including trade papers and web sites, as well as individuals who candidly share their impressions of a show on-line with their wide social networks.

As ticket prices have gone up, audiences have come to rely much more on word-of-mouth. They've also found that they can enjoy a show even if a critic didn't. So a show may do quite well despite getting mixed reviews.

Why do good shows fail? Every producer who doesn't have a hit will give you many different reasons to try to explain it. But the truth is that no one really knows what makes a hit. You can get terrible reviews from critics but audiences love it and keep it alive. On the other hand, your reviews can be great but the public doesn't buy it.

Sometimes audiences and critics both love a show – but it fails anyway. For instance, we produced *Gigi* – first trying it out at the Kennedy Center to see how well it worked. It ran for a month, received good reviews and sold out almost every show. Then, we made the decision to spend the rest of the money to bring it to Broadway – where it didn't fare well. Who knows why!

To this day I don't know what turns people on to one show or another. Show business is a crapshoot. You have to follow your intuition and passion, allow yourself to just jump in, and try to be okay with whatever happens.

Chapter 23
Is Show Business a Form of Gambling?

Another question I'm sometimes asked is whether producing is gambling? My answer is – not in my opinion.

Personally, I've never been drawn to traditional forms of gambling. To me, it is always simply and exclusively a way to make or lose a lot of money in a big hurry. When I tried gambling in casinos or such, I got very little thrill from it when I won and I felt really lousy when I lost.

One year, the Actors Fund had a "Gambling Night Charity Event," which I attended. When I entered the auditorium where it was held, I donated $1,000 and was given $1,000 worth of chips. I then walked through a large room containing many gift items from which to select – if you had any chips left at the end of the evening. The gifts were quite impressive, including trips to various vacation spots, suitcases, golf clubs, etc.

I spent the evening going from one gambling table to another. As strange as it seemed to me, I won at every table. The chips were piling up! The last table I visited was the craps table, where I stood next to the croupier. Because I knew nothing about the game, the croupier helped me place bets. I was having so much fun and winning so many chips, that I stayed until the end of the evening. When I collected and counted all of my chips at the end, I had about $10,000 worth and was looking forward to my prizes.

When I went into the Prize Room, however, all of the prizes that I'd seen at the beginning of the evening were gone. The attendant in the room felt so badly for me that he located an 8"x10" picture frame, which was all he had left. So my winning of $10,000 worth of chips wound up getting me a $10 picture frame. Fortunately, it was all for charity. As I said, I was never lucky at gambling for money.

So, in answer to that question I explain that to some people producing may be a lot like gambling. However, in the theatre business, there rarely are addicted gamblers.

For me, producing is a creative endeavor that can bring joy, laughter, and stimulation to everyone involved on both sides of the stage. It can have lasting, transformational effects on people. So, win or lose, I feel that I have accomplished something magical when I've produced a show − in addition to giving writers, actors, directors, designers, dancers, stage hands and all the other theatrical people a chance to succeed and make a name for themselves. How gratifying is that?!

Chapter 24
What Is the Role
of a Producer?

Another question I'm often asked is, "What does it take for a producer to put together a play or musical? What does he actually do?" Because it's such a major undertaking that requires several years of your life to accomplish, I'll provide an overview of the process over the next several chapters.

I've been producing for close to 40 years so there isn't much in the field that I haven't experienced. I've had hit shows and flops. There have been shows I've closed after Opening Night. I have more stories than I have time or space to cover here. So I just want to give an overall sense of what a producer does.

A producer is like the CEO of a big corporation and can begin a project in several different ways. The producer may be the initial creative force behind a show such that the idea and story for the show actually originate with the producer. Or the producer could find the script and develop it. Or the producer may be aware of a show in development, or playing at an out-of-town or off-Broadway theatre, and decide to get involved.

The producer (typically with one or more co-producers) acquires the rights to produce the show on Broadway (or elsewhere) from the author – as well as from the composer and lyricist if it is a musical. That's when the collaboration to bring the show to Broadway begins. The creative team is then hired – including the director, designers, choreographers, actors and others.

The producer does all the hiring and firing (except of the playwright who cannot be fired). The producer also leases the theatre and makes the hard decisions about how long to keep the show running if the costs are higher than the income it produces. The producer also decides on ticket prices, on an advertising and marketing team and budget, etc. In short, a producer makes all the decisions necessary for the show to be mounted and run.

Some shows close abruptly, as they quickly run out of money before building an audience. There are also shows that run for years but never pay back their initial investment. They just earn enough to run from week-to-week. A producer will run a show as long as possible because the longer it runs on Broadway, the more it is perceived to be a hit. When it is considered a hit, the value of the show is greatly increased, which hopefully ensures a long life *after* Broadway.

The rights to produce include the so-called ancillary and subsidiary rights. This means the show's company can even participate in the author's sale of the movie rights. This occurs when a movie producer or studio sees potential in turning the live show into a motion picture. The author may then sell these rights to the movie producer or studio. The show's company is typically entitled to receive about 40% of the money that the author receives for movie rights.

Ancillary rights also mean that the producer can take the show on a road tour across the United States and sometimes all over the world. To do so, the producer might hire a road tour agent to book many weeks at different theatres around the country and abroad.

A smart deal would provide that each theatre where the show plays agrees to pay the producer a guarantee to cover the costs of the show, plus a profit that varies at each venue. For example, a really big show might cost $400,000/week to run. So, the road theatre guarantees the $400,000 weekly expense plus a guaranteed profit of perhaps

$100,000/week. Or the theatre owner may pay a percentage of profits rather than the guarantee – or sometimes both, depending on the deal that is struck. Sometimes several theatres host the show in the same week. In booking terms, that's called 'split-weeks.'

This is not to say, however, that all shows that appear to be a hit can get a road tour. Road tour agents need enough theatres to want to book that particular show. It is mostly musicals that are popular for the road. Plays without a star very rarely tour.

Chapter 25
The Step-by-Step Production Process

My desk was always cluttered with scripts and musical tapes. These came to me primarily from agents, playwrights and friends, though many times they arrived unsolicited by mail.

When a script was submitted to me, I would read the first 10 pages. If it didn't appeal to me, I would pass on it unless, of course, it came from an important agent or playwright. Since they are the major source of product, and I was dealing with them continually, I would always read through the entire script as they would expect to have a discussion with me afterwards.

There are about five ways a producer gets involved in a project. The producer can –

1. **Find a script and take it from the page to the stage**. This was my favorite way.

2. **Do a revival of a successful play or musical**. This has definite advantages: The play has a proven track record and, if it is a musical, the songs are good. Then, all you need to do is bring

together a good cast, hire a good director, and create a good production team. Investors are a lot easier to find for revivals, as are stars, since they are already familiar with the project. The only catch here is that there is no guarantee that the show will be a hit this time around.

3. **Find a movie, adapt the story to the stage, or turn it into a musical.** *Pygmalion* turned into *My Fair Lady*. *Sunset Blvd.* came to Broadway as a musical from the movie. *Honeymoon in Vegas* and *Gigi* are two other examples of movies that were brought to the stage.

4. **Learn about a show playing in a regional theatre** somewhere in the country or the world and travel to see it. You might pick up the entire show and bring it to New York. London is a place where producers go every season for the purpose of finding shows to transfer to Broadway. The only show I brought from London was *Corpse* and it did fairly well.

5. **Come across a really good story or think up a good story yourself** and commission a playwright to write it for you.

Of the 40 shows I produced – 16 of which were musicals – some went from the page to the stage, some I brought to Broadway from elsewhere, and most were already heading for the stage and I was invited on as a producer.

Let me tell you how the process usually starts – though not necessarily always in the same order. Assuming you are the producer and have found a project you want to do, you must first secure the rights from the author. The rights are usually for a year or two with the option to extend, as you never really know how long it will take to put the show together. It can take two years but it can also take more.

The next step is to hire a General Manager who then prepares a budget for the show – whether it is a play or a musical. (After doing this for many years, I can envision the production while reading the script and also get a good sense of what the costs will be – including elaborate costumes, sets and special effects).

If you're doing a play, by union rules you know what the salaries are for the actors – though not for the stars or for that occasional actor who is not a star and yet gets more money. You also know the rent for the theatre.

As mentioned a few pages back, the budget for producing a play in 2015 was approximately $3,000,000. The budget for a musical, also around 2015, ran anywhere from $8,000,000 to $18,000,000.

After the General Manager reads the script, s/he completes the budget. Though the GM may originally allocate $500,000 for sets, nothing is set until the designer goes to the shop and comes back with an estimate.

Then it's time to find and hire the right director – and choreographer if one is needed – for a particular project. However, if the project was found at a regional theatre or somewhere else, you may decide to bring it to Broadway with the director, choreographer and cast intact.

If not, then a Casting Director must be hired to pursue the main star or stars for the show. This usually takes quite a bit of time as you can only go to one star at a time, then wait for that person to read the script and give you a time frame for their availability – if they're interested.

Reaching out to the stars: After reading the script, the producer and director discuss together who they think would be right to play a particular part. They then assemble a list of several possible candidates. Let's say, for example, that Julia Roberts is on the list of names.

They then go to the casting director and ask the CD to contact Julia Robert's agent to see if and when she might be available and what her rate would be. It may take Julia a month to read the script and determine if she would like to play this particular role on Broadway.

If she isn't interested, the Casting Director then goes through the same process with another actress on the list until one is found who is available and interested in accepting the part.

I was once trying to do a revival and we went to many stars but couldn't get one because we didn't have a theatre or a date. You really have to find out from the star when she or he wants to do the play. Then, you go to theatre owners for a date, which they can only provide if they have a show with a short run and a fixed closing date. Only then can you know when to build the sets and start rehearsals. I'll share more on the challenge of securing a theatre shortly.

If you don't have a star, casting can be done quite quickly. A casting call for union actors is advertised in all the trade papers. Perhaps 500 will people show up and the Casting Director then narrows it down to 3-4 people for every part. At that point, the author, director and producer watch their auditions, discuss their preferences, and make their selections.

Now you have the rights, the director, the casting director, the star and the other performers you want. The General Manager then follows-up with all the contracts.

Contracts are fairly standard. If an actor objects, you get another actor. Of course, it's a different story if you have a star.

Then, you continue building your team by hiring an advertising agency, a press agent, the designers for sound, lighting, sets and costume – plus the various other specialists required including special effects people, make-up artists, etc.

Chapter 26
Budgeting for Success

In the Appendices to this book you'll find a sample budget for a musical that includes all these line items and costs. This budget is based on a show that started out of town prior to coming to Broadway in 2015. If you were producing this show, this is how you could go about it.

After reviewing the budget and making cuts where possible, you'd arrive at the cost of the show. Then it's time to hire a theatrical attorney to prepare the offering papers so that you can go to investors and start raising the money. By law, you cannot spend any of the investors' money until you raise the entire cost of the production.

Once the company is formed, you cannot change the total budgeted in the offering papers. Therefore, as the producer, you must be sure you can bring the show in without going over budget.

The truth is, however, you're never really sure. It's only experience that helps you to become more accurate in your predictions. With *Daddy Goodness*, we made so many revisions to the show that we used up all our money with new sets and costumes and didn't have enough left to bring it to New York.

When you do a budget, you have to leave a good amount of money for reserves – because when you first open a show that doesn't have a star, you know you're going to lose money until the show builds – if it ever does. For example, you open a play and in the first week you may lose $70,000. In the second, you may lose $50,000, and in the third, you may lose $30,000. You have to be prepared to lose money for the first several months.

You may have allocated $1,200,000 for advertising. However, if you're running short of money because you didn't budget well, then you may have to cut back on your reserves and/or advertising. On the other hand, if you're lucky enough to sell a lot of tickets when you first open, then you won't have to touch your reserves.

A show may run for several years without really making a profit. It all depends on how many tickets you sell. It's possible to keep a show running as the ticket sales go down, using the reserves, so as to help the ancillary rights.

The longer you run the show the more likely it is to be perceived as a hit. Then, theatres across the country and around the world are more likely to want your show to travel to their venue.

Chapter 27
An Even Closer Look
at the Budget

If you look the 2015 production budget introduced in the prior chapter, you will see that the total minimum capital required was $11,000,000. However, the show would actually need to raise $12,750,000 for the producers to feel secure in having a contingency and reserve. Until the monies are raised and the partnership is closed, the up-front costs are covered by the producer.

On this particular budget, you will notice that the "Estimated Development Costs" were $155,000. These had to be advanced by the producer. This would be a total loss if the show did not proceed – either because the money could not be raised or for some other unforeseen situation that might occur.

Development costs can include hiring a general manager and a director and giving them money up front as a guarantee. If we were doing a Neil Simon play, back in his heyday, optioning the play could be very expensive. Hiring all the creative people would also cost money because no one will sign a contract without getting paid up front. This is because everyone is well aware that if the production team doesn't raise the investment capital, then the creatives would have invested their services without compensation. So you have to pay all your creative people up front because you are optioning their services and they cannot accept potentially conflicting work when they are under contract to you.

As you will see on the budget, the estimated fixed weekly operating costs for this sample Broadway production were $518,254. This does not include all of the royalties due, by contract, to certain people.

The royalties due are a percentage of the weekly adjusted gross receipts. Therefore, the dollar amount of royalties varies each week. The royalty percentages are fairly customary to the recipients and typically are the following percentages of the weekly adjusted gross receipts:

- The Producer's share is 3%
- The Composer's share is 2%
- The Lyricist's share is 2%
- The Author's share is 2%
- The theatre receives between 5-7%

Actually, the theatre royalty varies – usually depending on the size of the house. Houses on Broadway are categorized as musical houses and play houses. Small musicals can go into a playhouse because a big musical house may charge more money, or for other reasons.

If you have a star in a play, then you typically have to go into a larger house because the star will only give you a short run but will likely pull in a large audience. Fortunately, if you have what looks like a smash hit, and three theatre owners are competing for the show, then one of the theatre owners may charge you less.

All of this may vary depending on the theatre, the show, and the contracts that were made with the producer. Nothing is cut in stone in the theatre business. Everything is negotiable except union contracts. As for the bookkeeping, I'm happy to say that it is not the type of 'creative accounting' for which Hollywood is notorious.

Investors get 100% of the weekly net profits until their investment is fully paid back. This is an incentive that makes it possible to raise the money needed. The producers do not get any of the profits until after that point, and then the profits are shared 50-50 between the investors and the producers.

Once you raise all the money necessary to close the partnership, it's time to start the process. Setting a definite time frame is very important. Everyone's availability dates are needed in order to pick a time to start rehearsals, as well as to start building the sets and designing the costumes.

To avoid money and artistic pitfalls, you must decide whether or not you should take the show out of town for tryouts or aim directly for Broadway. The budget in the Appendix indicates costs for a show with an out of town tryout, followed by a transfer into Broadway.

Chapter 28
The Challenge of Securing the Right Theatre on Broadway

Every show has to wait for a theatre. And a producer must feel confident that s/he can secure the right-sized theatre for the show before beginning the process or the entire project could fall through.

A generally accepted rule of thumb for me is that a show should be presented in a venue where the show is bursting out of the theatre – where the stage and theatre seem even a bit too small for the show. This enhances the excitement and intimacy of viewing the show for the audience.

Perhaps you have seen a good show but were not thrilled by it. It's possible that it was in a space that was simply too large for that particular show. Musical houses are big and brash and you can be in a big house and still enjoy it. But an intimate play in a huge house isn't intimate any more.

Many of the 41 theatres on Broadway remain filled with hit shows from previous seasons. (For the past 30 years, *Phantom of the Opera* has occupied the Majestic Theatre). As a result, theatre owners are not always sure which of their bookings will close. And as previously mentioned, a theatre owner cannot ask a show to leave unless that show goes below a certain gross (ticket sales) for two consecutive weeks.

There are some shows, however, that are booked for limited runs. So in these cases, the closing dates are secure. Yet, with about 40 to 50 shows trying to reach Broadway each season, it could be difficult to get a commitment for the theatre you need.

The Helen Hayes is a perfect theatre for plays. Every actor loved playing our theatre. Ironically, however, there were only five shows that I was able to produce in my own theatre. Every time I had one ready, the Hayes was already booked so I had to take it elsewhere. The five shows I did produce there were *Torch Song Trilogy, Ned and Jack, Corpse, Getting and Spending,* and *George Gershwin Alone.*

Chapter 29
Scheduling Opening Night

Once a theatre has been booked for a show, the producer may figure on four weeks of rehearsals followed by three weeks of previews. So seven to eight weeks after the process begins, the show will be ready to open.

Some producers like to open right before the Tony's – like films that open close to Oscar time so they'll be 'top of mind' for Industry voters. As mentioned, the season runs from June to June – culminating sometime in June at the Tony's. So, as many as four shows could open in a single week late in the season. However, securing a date for opening night is not always so easy.

Only one show can open on any given night on Broadway. So, once the producers decide on their ideal opening night date, they have to get approval from the Broadway League, which books and controls the dates to avoid conflicts.

Though they often don't get to choose the day, some producers prefer opening on a Thursday night because then the reviews come out in the weekend papers. Some prefer Sunday night because if they get a review on Monday, and it isn't a great one, not too many people will pay attention to it. Other producers avoid Saturday if they're expecting really great reviews for that very same reason, which is that readers may not see it until Monday and then may tend to forget it.

If all the nights are already booked in a given week, then rehearsals have to go on for another week, which could throw the budget off. This brings up another important point to mention, which is that before even starting rehearsals the producer has to find a relatively inexpensive rehearsal space.

The show won't move into the actual theatre in which it will play until the previews begin. That's when it's possible to see how well everything works together on stage. Changes will likely be made all the way up to one or two days before opening night – at which point the producer or producers declare, 'I'm freezing the show.'

Chapter 30
The Opening Night Party
– And the Morning After

It has always been a tradition in the theatre business that every opening night show is followed by a party. Invited guests include everyone involved in the show— starting with the investors, their family and friends – as well as many people from the industry such as members of the Shubert, Nederlander, and Jujamcyn organizations. The parties are often extremely lavish and expensive with a guest list of 1,000 to 1,500 people at the total cost of $50,000-$150,000 depending on how lavish the party.

Needless to say, during my nearly forty years on Broadway, I have attended countless opening parties. I have also hosted numerous parties, as well. It's like being the father-of-the-bride – over and over again. It is always a fun evening, as you get to talk with all the show's performers and to mingle with the celebrities you invited to the show and, of course, to the party afterward.

In the pre-internet and cell phone days – when the *NY Times* theatre critic wielded the power to make or break a show on Broadway – producers and writers would wait nervously until around 11:30 in the evening when the press agent could get the early edition of the next morning's papers and bring the reviews to the party.

If the *Times* reviewer was even moderately enthusiastic about a show, one of the producers or the press agent would stand on a platform or chair and read the review out loud. If the *Times* gave the show a bad review, even though it didn't get read aloud, that silence thundered through the gathering and people started leaving early rather than partying into the wee hours of the morning.

The Morning After: The very next morning after opening night a meeting takes place at the advertising agency offices. Those attending are usually the producers, the general manager of the show, the advertising executives assigned to the show, and the press agent.

The press agent brings all of the print reviews, as this is the time when the producers make many decisions, such as: "Where do we advertise?" "How much do we spend on advertising?" and "How do we market and push the show forward?"

Then, a good part of the morning is devoted to looking for quotable statements among all the reviews. Each person at the conference table is given a stack of reviews and a marker pen. They read every review, whether good or bad, to select quotes that can be used in the advertising print, television, or other outreach materials including various flyers. If the show got good or mixed reviews, the choices of quotes is fairly easy.

In a bad review, the trick is to look for brief descriptions that sound impressive, such as: "Sets were fabulous," "Beautiful costumes," "Best dancing on Broadway." There may even be one particular actor that was "outstanding," even in a bad show, and that's a quote that can be used. After everyone at the meeting finishes reading the reviews and pulling their quotes, the decisions are made.

Chapter 31
What's the Best Way to Promote a Show?

All producers have different opinions about how best to promote a show. And there is no book that explains the best approach for any given situation.

Some producers choose to put a full-page ad in the *NY Times*. In 2015, the last time we had full-page ads running – for *Honeymoon in Vegas* and for *Gigi* – they each cost $75,000 for one day.

Some producers will only put a ¼ or ½ page ad in the paper. Some prefer to put their money on television ads. If you have a big star and what looks like a big hit, you may take two full pages of ads.

However, other producers with stars headlining their show say you don't need to take out ads. They reason that if you have a hit, you don't need to advertise. Word-of-mouth will do it for you. These days it's largely about the internet of course.

Sometimes you just listen to your ad agency because they may have the pulse of the public more fully than you do. Though you don't have to follow their recommendations, it pays to hear them out and then make your own decisions.

Chapter 32
David Merrick: The Great Promoter

There have been many producers before me and there will be many after. But no one will ever compare to the iconic showman David Merrick, the multi-award-winning producer and publicity prankster who ruled Broadway from the late 50's to the mid-80's with one success after another.[1] He died on April 25, 2000 at the age 88.

Merrick was always seeking headlines for his shows and was both inventive and outlandish in the lengths to which he'd go to attract publicity. In his career he produced approximately 90 shows and was known to have made huge profits. Among his successful musical hits were: *Gypsy,* starring Ethel Merman; *Hello Dolly!,* starring Carol Channing; *Promises, Promises;* and *42nd Street,* which at the time was the longest running show in Broadway history.

It was David Merrick who, in 1962, produced the musical, *I Can Get It For You Wholesale.* He cast an unknown 19-year old actress, Barbra Streisand, who went on to become a major star.

---

[1] Merrick went on to establish the David Merrick Arts Foundation in the late 90s to support the development of American musicals.

Merrick produced a show in 1949 called, *Clutterbuck*. In order to get publicity – beyond what the normal ways of advertising could produce – he called hotel bars and restaurants all over town each night at their busiest hours and would have them page a fictitious 'Mr. Clutterbuck' in order to create familiarity with that name. Perhaps because of that stunt he was able to keep the show open for another few months.

Several years later his show *Fanny*, which did not get favorable reviews, became a hit because of his tenacious and inventive ways of promoting it: He hired people to place stickers in men's rooms all over midtown Manhattan that read, "Have you seen *Fanny*?" He did radio and television spots using short vignettes from the show, which had not been done before. (Theatrical advertising agencies quickly followed suit). He was also the first producer to take a full-page newspaper ad for a Broadway show. *Fanny* consequently made a profit and ran for two years.

In 1957, Merrick's show, *Look Back In Anger*, was not doing well at the box office. During a performance an angry woman in the audience ran down the aisle and jumped on the stage at the Lyceum Theatre. She slapped one of the lead actors (Kenneth Haigh) for the negative statements his character made about women. Every newspaper ran the story for several weeks. The box office soared. Months later Merrick confessed that he had hired the woman for $250.

Merrick wasn't only a master at promotion. He took a creative leap when he successfully replaced the entire cast of *Hello, Dolly!* with an all black company starring Pearl Bailey and Cab Calloway. This was a highly successful move that helped to keep the show running when its audiences began to decline in 1967.

When Merrick saw little hope for his musical *Subways Are For Sleeping* in 1961, he found men in the phone book with the same names as the six or seven newspaper theatre critics. He invited them to dinner and then took them all to a preview of the show prior to the opening. The men all endorsed the show with such praises as, "the best musical of the century." Among the so-called 'critics' were a shoe salesman and a mailman.

Merrick then tried to take out a full-page ad showing rave reviews.

Though the *New York Times* rejected the ad, it did run in one edition of the *Herald Tribune* before the editors killed it. This publicity stunt got him international headlines and kept the show running for 205 performances, making for a profitable season.

I was at the opening of *42nd Street* in 1980. Gower Champion, the musical's director and choreographer had died early in the morning on the day of the opening, at age 59, of a rare blood cancer. No one in the audience had any knowledge of this since David Merrick kept the news secret from both the cast and reporters. He wanted to announce it from the stage at the curtain call. Along with the audience and the entire cast, I was stunned. The show's success was assured by the notoriety of Merrick's actions.

When the 1966 musical of Truman Capote's *Breakfast at Tiffany's* was previewing on Broadway, Mr. Merrick abruptly closed the show despite an advance sale of $1million. When asked why, he responded by saying, "I refused to subject theatregoers to an excruciatingly, boring evening." This can happen when what you conceive in your head about a show is not how it plays out. Merrick likely recognized that the show wasn't working and so cut his losses by ending it before its official opening. Audrey Hepburn, who had helped make the 1961 film adaptation so popular, was not in the play.

During the height of his career, Merrick was asked, "What's it like to be Number 1?" Here's how he responded:

> "I compare it to climbing Mt. Everest. It is very dif-
> ficult. Lives are lost along the way. You struggle and
> struggle and finally you get up there. And guess what
> is there when you get up there? Snow and ice."

Will there ever be another David Merrick on Broadway? I don't think so. Now it's the agencies that create the marketing strategies and the producer mostly just says Yes or No – based primarily on the budget. In Merrick's time, however, it was he who came up with publicity pranks that helped to assure the success of his shows and influence future marketing strategies.

Part III
A Glimpse into the Timeless

Chapter 33
Entertainers Never Die – They Just Slowly Fade Away

I wrote to Helen Hayes, as she hadn't come to the theatre for a period of time. She and her longtime friend, Lillian Gish, used to come together regularly to see most of the shows. Ms. Gish, known as the 'The First Lady of American Cinema,' was a wonderful stage and movie star for an astonishing 75 years (1912-1987. She died in 1993).

In my note to Ms. Hayes, I told her that we missed her and that her theatre was in good shape and running very well. I also reminded her of how proud I was to have her name on our marquee. She responded with a beautiful letter that, with the kind permission of the MacArthur Family Trust (Helen B. MacArthur, Trustee), you will find included in this chapter.

In most professions, people reach a certain age and then retire. That age varies, of course, with the profession and the person.

November 19, 1991

Dear Marty,

What delight you give me in your correspondence. As long as you send me such charming letters as on November 14th, I can never feel that my place in the New York Theatre is lost.

I did not mind giving up the work, but I was sad to lose my connection with the New York theatre, which has been my beloved home since I have been eight years old. Now if I feel lost, I can go down to 44th street and find my real home in the world.

One day I will call Susan Myerberg and make a date to come into town to pay a visit to all of you and to the pretty theatre.

Gratefully,

Helen Hayes

Performers tend to believe, feel (or hope!) that they are ageless. Many never stop looking for work. They refuse to grow old and usually believe in their ability to morph into whatever character they are playing. These optimists stay in touch with their agents – always hoping to get "that call."

There are innumerable examples of these talented diehards. For instance, Angela Lansbury, who won five Tony's, six Golden Globes, one Grammy, an honorary Oscar and an Olivier award, performed on Broadway in 2017 in *The Chalk Garden*. She is in her ninth decade. The beautiful Jane Fonda, now in her early 80s, is back doing TV and movies. Barbra Streisand, in her mid-seventies, is coming out of retirement. Tony Bennett never stopped working and is still singing and performing on stage at age 90. James Earl Jones is still doing Broadway in his 80s. And it was reported that Dick Van Dyke, at the age of 90, would be in the remake of *Chitty Chitty Bang Bang*.

I have some favorite stories I want to share with you about a few "old timers" I had the privilege of knowing.

Eubie Blake, an African American born in 1887, was one of the "never say die" breed. He was a director, composer and lyricist, whose unforgettable songs included "I'm Just Wild About Harry!" and "You Were Meant For Me." He wrote a Broadway musical in 1921, called *Shuffle Along*, which–played as a revival at Broadway's Music Box Theatre during the 2016 season.

Eubie was a member of the famed Friars Club, where he was honored on his 100th birthday. He sat at the piano, a cigarette dangling from his lips, a glass of scotch sitting on the edge of the piano, and spoke-sung some of his favorite songs.

I felt privileged to have been invited to his party. When the emcee asked Eubie what he owed his longevity to, the old-timer replied: "Beats me. But had I known I'd live to be 100, I would've taken much better care of myself!" Since I don't drink or smoke, I was inspired to believe that it should be easy for me, as well, to reach 100 years of age.

George Burns was another wonderful example of tireless talent. He was a household name for most of his long life – a huge success on stage, in movies and on television. Born in 1896, he was booked in

Las Vegas to perform on his 100th birthday. Unfortunately, he passed away right before the show could open.

George left them laughing right until the very end. He starred in a memorable movie, titled *Oh God!* when he was in his nineties.

The story I like the most about this theatrical icon happened when he was being interviewed at age 95. The interviewer asked if he was still sexually active. "Absolutely!" he replied. "Almost every night."

The interviewer almost choked. "Almost every night?"

Without blinking an eye George replied, "Yes. Almost Monday – almost Tuesday – almost Wednesday – almost Thursday – almost Friday. Weekends, I take a break."

And then we have Imogene Coca, who was born in 1908, and whose name was synonymous with comedy for many decades until her death at the age of 92. Her Saturday night television appearances with Sid Caesar on *Your Show of Shows* were a huge hit from 1950 to 1954.

Near the end of her life, a producer friend of mine cast her in one of his shows, which was touring the country. When I asked him how she was managing, he laughed.

> "She's blind in one eye and can hardly see in the other. She needs two strong men to get her onto the stage. But as soon as the curtain goes up, that old magic kicks in and she performs as if she were 25 years younger. Afterwards, this false youth evaporates, and she needs to be helped back to her dressing room."

Jerry Lewis was born in 1926. He and Dean Martin were the hottest act around for many years until their partnership broke up, shocking fans. Both of them went on to have very successful careers as independent performers.

Jerry Lewis was the Abbot of the Friar's Club in New York and, whenever possible, he attended their famous Saturday Brunch. I was lucky enough to be there when he came in with his entourage to celebrate his 90th birthday. While he sometimes used a walker, or on occasion, a wheelchair, when I last saw him at the Club, he was assisted by a helper.

He had just recently finished starring in the movie, *Max Rose*, which was released in 2016. In it, he played an aged pianist who learned that his recently deceased wife might have cheated on him in the early days of their marriage. Not bad to still be going that strong at 90 years of age!

When I was a young man enjoying a weekend at the Brown's Hotel in the Catskill Mountains of upstate New York, I learned that Jerry Lewis had worked as a waiter/busboy at that same hotel for several years before starting his career. He became very friendly with the owners and they would let him entertain once in a while. After his tremendous success with Dean Martin, he would return there on many occasions as a favor to the owners and give a performance.

I happened to be there when he was a guest of the hotel and had the privilege of spending an evening at the table with him and other entertainers. Seeing Jerry at the Friars Club and knowing that he still wanted to work was very gratifying to me. I was inspired by his vitality and his desire to continue working. I certainly hope to have that kind of strength well into my 90s.

Chapter 34
The Florida Follies – 2004

In 2004, I produced a musical revue at the Parker Playhouse in Ft. Lauderdale, Florida called *The Florida Follies*. The revue included singers, dancers, and various other acts.

The casting of the show was special to me as every performer had to be at least 65 years of age to qualify. I was amazed by how many entertainers showed up for the casting call.

We hired six dancers to form a chorus line, the youngest of whom was 68 and the oldest – 85. When the casting director first came to me and said, "We found an 85-year-old dancer," I joked, "That's great – but can she walk?"

When the chorus line started to tap dance with the 85-year-old dancer leading the way, audiences could not stop applauding. All the dancers were wonderful – as were the singers and the trainer in the dog act (the dogs, of course, were younger).

Florence Henderson, beloved as the mother in *The Brady Bunch*, which played on television from 1969-1974, was not only the Mistress of Ceremonies for the show, she sang and performed several numbers as well. She was in her seventies.

When it came to the old-time comedians, the laughter and response of our audience made my heart sing as they were obviously having a marvelous time. Since the show was mainly attended by the older generation, I suspect the jokes made our audience feel young again.

Every couple of weeks we had another celebrity perform as a special guest, such as Norm Cosby, Gertrude Lawrence, and Jack Carter. I'd hired the talented Carter to star as one of the headline comedians. He was 82 at the time and had a 20-minute stand-up routine.

Carter had been in show business since he was very young and was one of the top comedians of his day. He performed in every venue of show business including television, movies and Broadway along with doing stand-up comedy in nightclubs. He was still eager to perform and when he did, he had the audience laughing hysterically. They loved him.

On this occasion, however, I had a problem with Jack. Every night when he was scheduled to go on, I had to go into his dressing room and urge him to get up on his feet and go onto the stage. Each time he complained, "Marty, I can't make it. I feel faint and weak. I just can't perform tonight."

My response was always the same. "We have crowds of people who have come to see you, Jack. You can't disappoint them. Trust me, you'll feel better as soon as the curtain goes up. And so he'd do it – with someone assisting him onto the stage.

As soon as his act began, adrenaline immediately kicked in and each night he was dynamite up on stage – only to collapse when he returned to his dressing room. We went through this same routine nightly throughout his three-week booking.

That show really proved to me that when true performers are on stage, or in a movie, their passion for performing – and the adrenaline that kicks in to fuel them – are the secret ingredients in the "Fountain of Youth" that enable them to delight audiences till the end of their days.

Martin Markinson, Bob Cuillo, Michael Fuchs, Ellen M. Krass
Mort Swinsky, Elsa Suisman, Bernie Weintraub
in association with
Lawrence S. Toppall
Present

THE FLORIDA
FOLLIES

Bringing New Meaning To The Art Of Staying Young

Starring
Florence Henderson
Special Guest Stars
Norm Crosby • Carol Lawrence • Jack Carter
(Jan. 14 - Jan. 25)   (Jan. 28 - Feb. 15)   (Feb. 18 - Mar. 21)

Produced by   Executive Producer
Jean Ann Ryan Productions   **Ken Greengrass**

Featuring
Lorene Yarnell • Rio Clemente • Jan McArt
and
The Fabulous Darnells • Francois Szony & Rita Agnese • Sammy King

Barbara Bailey • Doug Crosley • Jim Franklin • Louise Farrand • Lorelie Lee
Liz Lieberman • Lynn Martin-Fouce • Bill Steele • Rudy Tronto • Betsy Wickard

Scenic Design **Tom John** Assistant Scenic Design **John Pollard** Lighting Design **James K. Ryan III**
Costume Design **Daniel Storey** Sound Supervision **Steve Weiss** Orchestrations **Johnny Harris**
Lyrics/Musical Direction **Dick Williams** Choreography **Jean Ann Ryan & Michael Kubala**
Executive Administrator **Kate Guimbellot** Technical Supervisor **James Ruth** Stylist **Robert Allen**
Associate Producer **Joanne Maiello** Company Manager **Cindy Wolf** Stage Manager **Amy London** General Manager **Lawrence Toppall**

Written and Directed By
Jean Ann Ryan

PARKER PLAYHOUSE • FT. LAUDERDALE

Part IV
Expanding My Reach

Chapter 35
Seduced by Evil: From Broadway Producer to Hollywood Filmmaker

It was 1996 and I was busy booking shows into the Helen Hayes Theatre while also looking for a play or musical that I personally wanted to produce for the stage. Then, something unexpected occurred.

My wife, Arlena, and I were at our home in Santa Fe, New Mexico when a friend of ours, Jann Arrington-Wolcott, was putting the finishing touches on a novel she was writing, titled *Brujo,* a Spanish word for a male sorcerer or witch doctor who works black magic.

It was an unusual story about a successful magazine publisher who lived and worked in Santa Fe, New Mexico. One of the main characters, Lee Lindsay, was a journalist as well as the wife of a prominent scientist and mother of a teenage daughter. Her well-ordered world was shattered when she traveled to an isolated mountain village to interview Juan Mascarenas, a local historian and rumored healer or *curandero.*

The village seemed strangely deserted when Lee arrived and the charismatic Mascarenas was not at all what she expected. The interview quickly took a shocking turn that would confuse and haunt Lee in the days to come. Inexplicable things began to happen. She experienced strange flashbacks to what may have been a past life as a Pueblo Indian. An ominous raven appeared, watching her day-by-day and invading her dreams at night. Surprising sexual obsessions turned to terror and Lee had to find a way to fight unseen and unknown forces to save herself, her marriage, and the lives of those she loved.

Jann asked my wife to look it over, give her opinion and make suggestions. After reading the manuscript, Arlena suggested that I read it, too, as she felt it could make a good movie. I stared at her. "Make a movie? What the hell do I know about making movies?"

Arlena laughed. "What the hell did you know about owning a theatre or producing shows on Broadway? And look at what you've accomplished!"

So I read the book, found it mesmerizing, and agreed that it could, indeed, make a thrilling movie.

I spoke to Jann and told her what I thought, so she happily gave me the option for the movie rights. She was beyond excited because, although she was a seasoned journalist, *Brujo* was her first attempt at fiction.

I tried to figure out my next move. There was a talented screenwriter in town with whom I was friendly so I asked him to read the book and give me his opinion about its viability as a movie. He shared my enthusiasm. So, I asked him if he would write the screenplay on "spec," which means I wouldn't pay him for doing it, but if it turned out well, he would be attached as the screenwriter.

Since he was a member of the Screenwriters Guild, he told me he would have to charge me his minimum fee of $35,000. I wasn't interested in investing that kind of money just to see if he could write a good enough screenplay. So, I decided to drop the project for the time being and try to figure out another approach.

Three or four months later, he called to say that Jann's story kept going around and around in his head and he now agreed to write it for me on spec. It turned out to be a good script, and we decided to proceed and try to get a movie made.

The agent for the screenwriter sent the script around and it was optioned by Wilshire Court Productions, a branch of Paramount Pictures, and sold to USA Cable to be filmed as a T.V. movie. Happily, the author and screenwriter both got their fees and I was paid as executive producer.

We were now on our way to production! There were, however, two caveats that USA Cable insisted on. One was the name of the film. They felt that much of the public would not know what a "brujo" was or what it meant, so they changed the name of the movie to *Seduced by Evil*. We were so ecstatic that the film was going to be made that we didn't care what they called it.

The other caveat was that, although the story took place in and around Santa Fe, New Mexico, they needed a "Right to Work" state, as they wanted to use some non-union workers, which would be illegal in New Mexico. So the entire production was moved to Tucson, Arizona.

The next step was for USA Cable to decide on casting. Suzanne Somers had long been fascinated by Northern New Mexico's ancient tri-cultural history and archeology (Native American, Hispanic, and Anglo). She also had great appreciation for the areas' stunning vistas and expressed interest in the movie when asked.

When I told our friend Jann that Somers had been chosen to play the lead, she laughed. "That makes perfect sense," she said. "While I was writing the story, I took frequent breaks to exercise with Suzanne's "Thigh Master" equipment. So she's been part of this project all along!"

As mentioned, I became the Executive Producer and spent a lot of time on the set where I watched and learned the disjointed way a movie is made. They may shoot pages 3-4 of the screenplay on one day and pages 20-21 the next day – depending on an actor's parts.

For example, if an actor plays in only two or three non-consecutive scenes, they may shoot those scenes in just a couple of days. That way, the actor can leave rather than stay on the set for the entire shoot, which can last many weeks. The movie is actually put together in the editing room. It was a totally different experience from producing a play.

Seduced by Evil played on the USA Cable Network on and off (especially near Halloween) for many years and did well as a feature film in Spain and other Spanish-speaking countries.

Jann Arrington-Wolcott's novel was actually printed and published after the movie was released and it sold to rave reviews internationally—a most unusual experience for a first-time novelist. "I'm still riding high on that thrilling experience," she told me recently. "You changed my life, Marty. After all these years, I still get fan letters and requests for a *Brujo* sequel. I'm going to have to live a long time to write all the books that are in me."

After *Brujo* was published, I agreed to Jann's request to interview me at a writer's conference about making a movie from a novel. Afterwards, the sizable crowd went wild. Almost every writer attending was clamoring for my attention, hoping I could do the same for their novel. I barely got out of there in one piece. That's when I realized I had to keep a low profile to avoid being so inundated by the movie business or I'd have little time to get back to Broadway.

So, what else did I learn from that movie-making experience? I now understood the different kinds of pressure it puts you under compared to producing a live show. I was accustomed to being in control on Broadway and found it unnerving that – due to shooting the movie out of context – I never knew what we were getting until the final editing was done.

I quickly tired of changing locations so often, with all the chaotic movement and unforeseen happenings that occurred. I much preferred working in theatre where you live in one building with a controlled environment and only a few scene changes.

I knew that if I ever tried my hand at filmmaking again, I would have to be the primary producer with the power to make my own decisions. As it turned out, a screenplay that really grabbed me was sent to me the very next year.

Suzanne Somers starring in *Seduced by Evil*

Chapter 36
Snitch – the Movie

Snitch, a detective story, was originally written as a play by two very talented writers, George K. Cybulski and W. Colin McKay. They then decided it would be even better as a movie, so they wrote the screenplay.

I had a producing partner for movies named Richard Polak and we both liked it and agreed that it looked reasonable to produce. So, we optioned it and wasted no time getting started.

Since we'd never done a movie budget before, we hired a "Line Producer," which is similar to a General Manager on a Broadway show. We were told that we could do this movie as a low-budget production. That meant we could shoot it in 30 days using no more than 10 locations for a budget of between $1,000,000 and $1,200,000.

Polak and I believed we could do this ourselves – raise the money, do the hiring, and be independent producers. My son, Keith Markinson, had graduated from Emerson College with a major in Editing and Film. He was working in Hollywood as a film editor at that time. So, we hired him as our director and editor.

We then hired a casting director to handle the casting – subject to our final approval, of course. It took some time to get a complete cast together, however it ultimately turned out to be a very good cast despite the low budget.

If fact, we got really lucky! One day, the casting director called us to say that he'd heard Marlee Matlin had just gotten out of the hospital after giving birth and was looking for a project.

This was a great stroke of luck as Matlin is an Oscar winner for her performance in Mark Medoff's movie, *Children of a Lesser God*. Polak and I liked her work and agreed that she would be perfect for the starring role in *Snitch*. A script was sent to her and she liked it so well that she immediately accepted the part.

While all of this was going on, we were busy raising the $1,200,000 needed to close the deal. I was getting more excited every day, eager to put into practice all that I had learned while acting as Executive Producer on *Seduced by Evil*. Now, I was set to become an actual producer[2] on this new film – making all the decisions along with my partner, and working directly with my son, Keith.

What I didn't know was how hard and nerve-wracking it is to produce a low-budget film. Every dollar counts. And filming at many different locations is an exhausting challenge involving frequent moving, building sets, and getting it all set up. Most days turned out to be 15-hours long. And we never knew if we could have the same location for the next day. We were a non-union production which provided more flexibility to keep us within budget.

In spite of the hurdles, we were moving along on schedule. We had to check the "dailies" each evening to be certain we didn't have to re-shoot any scenes. "Dailies" are all the scenes that were shot that day. By reviewing them, the film editor and production team can be certain that they have enough good footage to put the movie together.

All the actors were responding very well to the speed and smoothness of the shoot without any major problems. Then, one day, I arrived at the set at my usual time, 6 a.m., dressed in jeans and a casual work

[2] The executive producer is essentially a co-producer – someone who is involved but has no decision-making authority. The actual producer makes all the decisions – though the studio can override the producer.

shirt. Before I was even out of the car, I saw the director (my son, Keith) striding toward me.

"Dad! We're prepared to shoot a scene we set up last night in this hotel lobby. It's designed as a bus stop where an older gentleman gets his pocket picked by a young man. But we have a problem. The actor playing the older guy had to have two wisdom teeth pulled out yesterday on an emergency basis, and his face is blown up like a balloon. He can barely speak. Since you're the only other older man on the set, we need you to get to Makeup and Wardrobe immediately. Here are your six lines. Please start memorizing them!"

I was too rushed to get nervous – until I realized the lines weren't sticking in my head. Then, the nervousness set in. We did the first take and I blew it – I missed the mark where I was meant to stand. The second take wasn't much better, as I turned the wrong way. On the third take, I got the business right – standing where I was supposed to stand and facing whom I was supposed to face. But I blew my lines.

Keith tried to calm me down. "Dad, relax. You can do this. Just take some deep breaths and we'll try again."

The fourth take was an improvement, but not good enough. After more deep breaths, we went for the fifth take. Finally, I got it all right and heard those welcome words, "Okay! That's a wrap!"

The relief I felt was enormous and most satisfying. I then realized that everyone on the set had been watching me. I stepped off the set to thunderous applause. Marlee Matlin rushed over to give me a big hug and I received congratulations from everyone. The director had a huge smile on his face. "Great, Dad! You saved the day!"

For the first time in my theatrical life, I understood the stage fright that so many actors go through – as well as the exhilaration that makes it all worthwhile.

Now that I was actually in a movie with a speaking part, I became eligible to join SAG, the Screen Actor's Guild. It didn't take me long to decide that *Snitch* would be my one and only acting gig, so I declined.

After 30 days, the shoot was complete – on time and on budget. Then came the process of editing, which can make or break a movie. Once that was complete, I felt a father's pride when everyone involved with the movie agreed that it was both well directed and well edited.

Next came the challenge of trying to sell the movie. We showed it around and ended up hiring one of the top agencies that sell and promote independent films. They held special screenings for distributors, studios and other independents. Unfortunately, this didn't succeed in creating enough interest. So, we decided to leave the agency and see what we could do on our own.

We displayed the film at a foreign film convention in Hollywood and were able to sell the foreign rights. We were also successful in selling it to various video stores such as Blockbuster, Hollywood Video, and Hastings. That meant we were able to recoup our initial investment.

The whole process was a tremendous learning experience. Despite all the anxiety, it was a great deal of fun. And I was happy with what we had accomplished even though we didn't have a theatrical release. Our movie came out in 2001 and, in addition to Marlee Matlin, featured William McNamara and Mariette Hartley.

william mcnamara
marlee matlin
snitch
CINESTAGE PRODUCTIONS presents a MARKINSON/POLAK PRODUCTION of a KEITH MARKINSON film
MARLEE MATLIN WILLIAM McNAMARA "SNITCH" TISHA CAMPBELL JAY ACOVONE and MARIETTE HARTLE
Casting by DONALD PAUL PEMRICK & DEAN FRONK costume designer CHARLES E. WINSTON
production designer MARTINA BUCKLEY music by JOSEPH WILLIAMS director of photography DARKO SUVAK
executive producers ROBERT ALSCHULER & SUSAN ALSCHULER associate producer MARTIN KATZ
co-producer RITA ROKISKY produced by MARTIN MARKINSON & RICHARD POLAK
written by GEORGE K. CYBULSKI & W. COLIN McKAY based on their play "SNITCH"
directed and edited by KEITH MARKINSON
© CINESTAGE PRODUCTIONS. All Rights Reserved

SNITCH: ON THE SET, APRIL 1996[3]

Richard Polak,
Marlee Matlin,
Martin Markinson

Keith Markinson,
William McNamara,
Martin Markinson

Martin Markinson
dressed for the shoot

Martin Markinson
in the bus scene

Richard Polak,
Tisha Campbell,
Martin Markinson

Mariette Hartley

Keith Markinson, Director, working on set

Keith Markinson and Marty Markinson

Chapter 37
Getting and Spending: Don't Count Your Ducks Till They're in the Pond

After *Snitch* I still had the "movie bug." The following-ing year, 1998, a playwright, Michael Chepiga, sent me a play titled *Getting & Spending*. It was an intriguing and timely story about a beautiful woman, a partner in a Wall Street firm, who is being indicted for insider trading.

I definitely wanted to produce this play on Broadway. Just as important, however, I saw the potential for a good movie. I approached the author, who had never had a play on Broadway and told him I would do the play only if he gave me the movie rights up front. We made a deal in which I optioned the play and movie rights at the same time.

I wanted to first try the show out of town to see how it played. Was it Broadway-worthy? If not, I would continue with just trying for a movie. I sent the play to the Old Globe Theatre in San Diego, CA. After a few months, they said they would do the play but if I wanted the sets and costumes to be Broadway quality, I would have to financially enhance the production myself, which I did.

The show turned out well and received good reviews. Fortunately, my theatre became available just as we concluded the Old Globe run so it worked out perfectly. The move from the Old Globe to the Helen Hayes worked well and the show ran for 3-4 months. Then I was ready to pursue it as a film and needed someone to write the screenplay.

Michael Chipega, the author of the play, said he would like to try his hand at doing just that. I agreed, providing he would do it "on spec." I would give him credit as the screenwriter if it came out well. I encouraged him to find a collaborator who had written screenplays before. He said he had just the right person in mind. So the screenplay was written and I felt it was very good.

I then spent time in Hollywood, pitching the movie to various agents and production companies. All to no avail. One day, sometime later, I was describing the story to someone who said she had a good contact that might be interested. After reading the screenplay and liking it, she instructed me to send it to Milkwood Films, Catherine Zeta Jones' production company.

Milkwood liked it and I was delighted to hear that Catherine wanted to star in it. They optioned the rights from me and it looked like we were on our way. I was especially encouraged as Zeta-Jones kept asking for re-writes. The writers were, of course, happy to accommodate her.

The company had the rights for one-and-a-half to two years. However, Milkwood couldn't find the full financing and finally dropped the project even though it had been announced in *Variety* (April 14-20, 2003 issue). The *Variety* article, dated April 9, 2003 from London by Stuart Kemp, entitled "Pathe 'Spending' with Zeta-Jones", described the production as a joint venture of Milkwood Films with Pathe Pictures, the UK company operated by French-owned Pathe Entertainment and US-owned Starboard Entertainment, and named me as executive producer. It quoted Pathe U.K.'s managing director describing the movie as "a wonderfully clever romantic comedy"; and also quoted Ms. Zeta-Jones: "I have had a longtime interest in the material and am looking forward to its fruition."

After that big disappointment, I did find an experienced and respected director who wanted to direct the movie. Knowing that Hollywood projects often take many years to come to fruition, I left it in his hands. I would speak to him from time to time and receive his assurances that he hadn't given up on it.

As for me, my time chasing movies in Hollywood ended with this drawn-out episode. Shooting out of context, looking at the dailies to see if the filming went well, and then not knowing how it would all come together until the editor put it together – I found it too unnerving. It was not nearly as much fun for me as producing a show for Broadway.

Ge†ting And $pending

Martin Markinson, Elsa Haft, Allen M. Shore,
Xorma Langworthy, Sheilah Goldman

PRESENT

Getting and $pending

BY Michael J. Chepiga

STARRING

Linda Purl   David Rasche

WITH

MacIntyre Dixon   Jack Gilpin   Deirdre Lovejoy
Debra Mooney   Derek Smith

SCENIC DESIGN	COSTUME DESIGN	LIGHTING DESIGN	SOUND DESIGN
James Xoone	Michael Krass	Kevin Adams	Jeff Ladman

CASTING	PRESS REPRESENTATIVE	PRODUCTION STAGE MANAGER	PRODUCTION SUPERVISOR
Elissa Myers C.S.A. Paul Fouquet C.S.A.	The Pete Sanders Group	Kelley Kirkpatrick	Gene O'Donovan

MARKETING	ADVERTISING	GENERAL MANAGEMENT
The Richards Group	LeDonne, Wilner & Weiner Inc.	Brent Peek Productions

DIRECTED BY

John Tillinger

Helen Hayes Theatre
240 WEST 44TH STREET

Chapter 38
California, Here I Come! The Wadsworth Theatre – 1998

While we were preparing to film *Snitch,* my son Keith was friendly with a young man named Rich Willis who was an aspiring actor and stuntman for the movies. As a result of their friendship, I gave Rich a small part in the movie and got to know him over time.

We spoke about my work in New York as a theatre owner and producer. He told me that there was a theatre in Los Angeles on the property of the Veterans Administration called the Wadsworth. It had been used by the University of California at Los Angeles (UCLA) as an entertainment and education venue for many years. It happened that their lease was over and the VA was looking for someone to advise them as to what kind of lease would serve them best, what that lease should contain, and appropriate fees for the rental.

I called the proper party at the VA, introduced myself, and said I would be happy to consult with them. After learning about my background, they were eager to set up a meeting and to give me a tour of the theatre. I was surprised and impressed to find a recently refurbished and almost complete operating theatre with 1,400 seats. It was similar in size and shape to many Broadway houses used for musicals and large plays.

I learned that UCLA had been paying them only $12,000 annually for the use of the theatre. I was astonished that they received such a small rental for such a beautiful venue.

The VA wanted to send it out for bids and asked me to help them. When I advised them on what they could actually charge for leasing the theatre, they asked if I would be interested in making a bid and sending in a proposal.

Always open to new ideas, I started to give it some thought. At the time, I was producing two movies and had a third one under option. Did I really want to continue on the very frustrating path of trying to stay in the film business? Or would I rather have another, much larger theatre in which to produce plays and musicals?

I decided to do the 'due diligence' needed by studying the world of theatre in Los Angeles before making that decision. I learned that aside from many small theatre venues with 100-250 seats, there were only three major theatre operations in L.A.

At the time, the Nederlander Organization owned and operated the Pantages Theatre, which is a large venue that books hit Broadway musicals. The Ahmanson Theatre Group had three or four different sized theatres and a very large subscription base from which they received revenue. As a nonprofit, they were also able to receive donations and funding.

Another non-profit theatre company, the Geffen Playhouse, had two venues, one being a 500-seat house. They also had a large subscription base and produced several of their own shows per season.

I also learned that the Shubert Organization had recently closed the very large Shubert Theatre in Century City.

Before I would submit a bid to the Veterans Administration for the Wadsworth, I had to come up with additional ideas for the use of the theatre that would make it work financially and enable me to compete with the others. My brain was racing.

Because of the nature of the VA property, I would have the use of an outdoor parking lot that could hold 500-700 vehicles. There were lovely grounds, where I envisioned lawn parties for fund-raising organizations. I felt that I could utilize these attractions to my advantage in addition to staging theatrical shows.

I submitted my bid and proposal highlighting the potential profit the VA could realize, which was far in excess of what UCLA had been paying them for years. I waited for their response for several months and after not hearing from them for that long, assumed they went elsewhere.

Finally I heard from the VA that they had accepted my bid. We started negotiations and in 1999 signed a lease, which they called a "sharing agreement," to expire in January 2003. I hired Rich Willis, the young man who had introduced me to the VA, to run this California operation and together we started to plan how we wanted to proceed.

The theatre, which was built in 1939 in the Spanish Colonial Revival style, needed very little refurbishment. I wanted to rename it 'The Bob Hope Theatre' but the VA thought they had an obligation to maintain the Wadsworth name.

We came up with a plan to incorporate a variety of uses for the facility, including:

1. Broadway shows
2. Film premieres/screenings
3. Film and TV location shoots
4. Concerts/children's theatre
5. Symposia
6. Lawn Parties for various charities

We started by leasing the theatre to a church group to have their services there every Sunday. They were a large congregation and 1,400 seats served them well. The lease agreement had a clause stating that they must clear the theatre by 1:00 PM every Sunday if we had a show with a 3:00 PM curtain.

We then granted a lease to a temple that needed the use of all the seats for two weeks each year on the Jewish High Holy Days.

Broadway shows were next. Some of these we produced ourselves and some were brought to us by other producers for short-term runs. These included Bea Arthur in *Concert*; *Bronx Tale*, starring Chaz Palmiteri; a concert version of Stephen Sondheim's *Follies*; *Salome*, starring Al Pacino and Jessica Chastain; Jackie Mason and his one man show; *Golda's Balcony* written by William Gibson and starring Tovah Feldshuh, which played at the Wadsworth after its successful run at the Helen Hayes; plus *Hair* – to name just a few.

I started to produce a show titled *The Gathering* by Arje Shaw, starring Hal Linden. I decided to try it out at the Wadsworth and then move it to the Parker Playhouse in Florida before moving it to Broadway. There was only one snag: The Helen Hayes was booked at the time. So I had to go into a Shubert House. This happened frequently with some of the shows I produced because the Hayes was booked most of the time.

A magician/illusionist named Criss Angel, who had been working in live theatre and television, wanted to book the Wadsworth for a private workshop where he could develop his illusions on a large stage in a big theatre. We gave him a lease for several months. He brought in his magic team, which included Stan Winston and his famous robots, as well as the highly regarded lighting designer, Jules Fisher.

Las Vegas organization's like Bally's, Cirque du Soleil and the Steve Wynn Resorts Company were eager to see the illusionist perform live while they considered presenting Criss Angel in their Las Vegas venues. Criss's extensive pitches to each entity had been done in their offices and this private workshop presentation would prove that the illusions worked in a live theatre. Ultimately, Criss concluded a deal with Cirque du Soleil and his show has been running with Cirque in Las Vegas since 2008

We then proceeded to make contact with several party planners who did major parties for movie and TV studios. When they came to see our facilities, they were amazed at what could be done. We then began booking film premier parties and screenings of new films.

The studios started to book the Wadsworth not only for screenings but also rented our parking lot for their enormous parties. They would cover the entire parking lot with a tent almost the size of a football field. The bookings were typically for five or six days – three days to set up, one night for the party and two days to take it down. Their screening and party cost them between $1,000,000 to $1,500,000, which also included our rental fees for five days.

We leased the property for many of these screenings and parties. To name just a few:

- Columbia Pictures: *Spiderman*
- New Line Pictures: *Lord of the Rings*
- Dreamworks: *Small Time Crooks* by Woody Allen
- Warner Brothers: *Divine Secrets of the YaYa Sisterhood*
- HBO TV Series: *Rome*

We also gave UCLA a four-year lease to continue their Sneak Preview classes at the Wadsworth. They were accustomed to screening new movies that were followed by discussions with notable guest speakers like the director, producer and star. This enabled the major studios and independents to get a sense of audience opinion.

Once word got out in the industry of our space and activity, we started to get film and TV location shoots. Among them were:

- Columbia Pictures, *The Wedding Planner*, starring Matthew McConaughey and Jennifer Lopez.
- ABC's *Partridge Family*
- Warner Bros' *Beautiful* directed by Sally Field.

We also did many concerts, Children's Theatre, and benefits, including –

- The Natural Resources Defense Council's Bi-annual Benefit, starring President Bill Clinton, Tom Hanks, Dustin Hoffman, Leonardo Di Caprio, Cameron Diaz, Larry David, and hosted by Robert Kennedy, Jr.

- Raffi, Children's Theatre, presented by House of Blues.
- Theodore Bikel in Concert.
- Crossroads School Benefit, starring Dustin Hoffman, Jim Belushi, Ted Danson, and Mary Steenburgen
- Debbie Allen Dance Academy
- And symposia held by Microsoft, Virgin Atlantic Air, the FBI, and the Screen Actors Guild.

We were also the site of many lawn parties for charities in the area.

All of this programming at the theatre and the surrounding grounds made us very successful. Just the movie premiers alone were making us a lot of money.

Being bi-coastal with all this success was very gratifying for me. The plan I envisioned put us on the map in Los Angeles. The thought of doing movies in Hollywood never even came up again for me. However, if one of my movie scripts were ever optioned – I might have reconsidered.

Our success continued to grow and Rich Willis, the employee who started with me, was very instrumental in creating all this programming for us. As a result, I made him an equal partner in the California operation. I will always be grateful for his foresight and invaluable contributions.

APRIL 14 – MAY 14
26 PERFORMANCES ONLY

AL PACINO

KEVIN ANDERSON
JESSICA CHASTAIN
ROXANNE HART

in a PRESENTATION WITH MUSIC of
OSCAR WILDE'S MASTERPIECE

SALOME

DIRECTED BY ESTELLE PARSONS

"A SMASHING, LUXURIOUSLY
ENTERTAINING NEW PRODUCTION
that chills even as it generates heat. With both a
scary emotional intensity and a pitch-black sense of
humor, the performances makes *Salome* as luridly
immediate as this morning's tabloids.
INSPIRED AND SEXY
AS ALL GET-OUT."
- BEN BRANTLEY, *THE NEW YORK TIMES*

"WHAT A HOOT!
A MESMERIZING, PRODUCTION
that defiantly and outrageously crosses the line
from the impossible to the brilliant.
Yes folks, AL PACINO IS BACK."
- LINDA WINER *NEWSDAY*

" MY ADVICE? DON'T MISS SALOME.
This may be a once in a life time chance."

- LIZ SMITH

213-365-3500 or ORDER ONLINE AT *ticketmaster.com*

OPENING NIGHT • APRIL 24, 2001 • the gathering

He couldn't change the past. But he would never forget it.

HAL LINDEN in
the
gathering
A NEW PLAY BY ARJE SHAW
directed by REBECCA TAYLOR

MARTIN MARKINSON LAWRENCE S. TOPPALL BRUCE LAZARUS DANIEL S. WISE MARTHA R. GASPARIAN STEVE ALPERT ROBERT MASSIMI in association with DIASPORA PRODUCTIONS present HAL LINDEN in THE GATHERING a new play by ARJE SHAW with MAX DWORIN SAM GUNCLER DEIRDRE LOVEJOY COLEMAN ZEIGEN scenery by MICHAEL ANANIA costumes by SUSAN SOETAERT lighting by SCOTT CLYVE sound by T. RICHARD FITZGERALD sound effects by JEREMY M. POSNER music by ANDY STEIN casting LAURIE SMITH production stage manager DOM RUGGIERO production management JUNIPER STREET PRODUCTIONS general manager ROGER ALAN GINDI press representative KEITH SHERMAN & ASSOCIATES associate producers MICHAEL W. GOLDSMITH ELSA DASPIN HAFT ESTHER SHAW directed by REBECCA TAYLOR

CORT THEATRE 138 W 48th Street Tele-charge 212-239-6200

Chapter 39
Ft. Lauderdale, Florida – The Parker Playhouse

In the fall of 2000, I received a call from a producer friend of mine who lived part-time in Ft. Lauderdale, Florida. He asked if I had any interest in operating a theatre there. My mind went into high gear. Since I had a theatre in California and one on Broadway, this would give me the option to move shows around the country to my own houses rather than renting from others.

I thought about the history of the Parker Playhouse. It had opened in 1967 and had the distinction of being the only major theatre in all of south Florida at the time. It had 1,162 seats, which gave it the ability to house musicals as well as plays. It was considered one of the most beautiful, well-maintained theatres of its day and one of the prime theatres in the country. Since every producer wanted to have their shows play in south Florida, the Parker was a destination point for touring shows from Broadway.

Many years ago, more plays than musicals opened on Broadway. This was back in the days when movie stars used to perform a great deal on Broadway and would then continue with the show while touring the country. As a result, many top stars, including the likes of Richard Burton, Elizabeth Taylor, Kathryn Hepburn, Carol Channing, Christopher Plummer and Judy Holliday—to name just a few—were frequent Broadway performers.

Unfortunately, things changed on Broadway. Eight shows a week was a grind for most stars, plus Broadway wasn't nearly as profitable when they could do a movie and quickly make millions. For instance, when Robin Williams performed, on stage, he made $100K a week doing eight shows a week. On a movie, he could make $10-15 million in two months. Therefore, road tours for plays without stars dwindled very fast all over the country. That's when the Parker started to suffer financially.

Shortly afterward, a non-profit theatre company built the Broward Center for the Performing Arts in Ft. Lauderdale, which opened in early 1991. They were able to get financial backing and very quickly developed a large subscription base, which enabled them to attract hit musicals from Broadway, guaranteeing the producers a profit. The Parker then lost the status of being a prime theatre. It remained open for many years but was no longer successful.

I was intrigued by the possibility of leasing the Parker and trying to regain its lost prominence. So, in 2000, I leased the theatre for six years and started to bring in popular shows from all over the country that were not as expensive to produce but could still fill a theatre that size. I also leased out the theatre for various events.

I now had the ability – when I produced a show for Broadway – to try it out first at the Wadsworth in Los Angeles, then at the Parker in Ft. Lauderdale, and finally on Broadway if it proved good enough. I was very successful in doing that shuffle with *The Gathering* starring Hal Linden, but not with every show.

From 2000 to 2006, some of our most successful shows at the Parker were *The Sunshine Boys*; *The Odd Couple*; *Defending the Caveman*; *Golda's Balcony*; *Dame Cora*; *Dirty Blonde*; and *Florida Follies*. These all became successful for me.

There were many other shows that were not financially successful. So, when the lease at The Parker was up in 2006, I realized that my time, effort, and financial resources were too much at risk to continue.

In addition, the competition with the Broward was becoming too stressful and was taking me away from producing in New York. So I decided not to renew the lease for the Parker Playhouse.

This experience taught me that trying to bring a theatre back to its original prominence was a risky business in a new era. Sometimes you can't resurrect or remake a time that has passed.

Chapter 40
Los Angeles, California –
The Brentwood Theatre

In 2003, we found a building located on the same large VA property that was not being used. We saw an opportunity to refurbish and convert it into a small 500-seat theatre—similar to the Helen Hayes on Broadway. The VA gave us permission to renovate the building and we immediately started construction – finishing the $1,000,000 makeover a year later. The building had been called the Brentwood. We renamed it the Brentwood Theatre.

We then got a call from the Geffen Theatre Group wanting to lease the Brentwood Theatre for a year, as they were preparing to do a major renovation on their own theatre in Westwood near UCLA. Being a non-profit and having a major list of subscribers, they needed a place for their upcoming season. We gave them a lease for a year, which covered almost our entire cost of construction. When their lease expired in 2005, we then started to lease and produce shows that were better served in a 500-seat house than the much larger Wadsworth.

Souvenir had opened on Broadway (I was not the producer when it did). After its run I moved and produced the show at the Brentwood Theatre.

The Two and Only opened at the Brentwood and then moved to Broadway.

My Mother's Italian, My Father's Jewish, and I'm In Therapy. After playing the Brentwood, this show toured the country.

The Brentwood Theatre was also a successful venue and we were then able to re-negotiate our entire lease (called a "Sharing Agreement") with the VA for 20 years, expiring in December 2024.

Chapter 41
Always Expect the Unexpected – So Long, Wadsworth Theatre

In the summer of 2008, the Veterans Administration claimed they were receiving complaints from veteran's organization. The complaint was that veterans in recovery programs on the premises of the VA should not be forced to watch the consumption of alcohol in direct proximity to their programs.

They informed us that we could no longer serve alcohol at any event that we held on the premises of the VA. This would mean that we could no longer attract movie premieres or lawn parties, which were a major source of income for us. The VA also imposed other new conditions, which we viewed as major restrictive changes to our contract. As a result of these restrictions, we would not be able to service our debt or gain an investment return on the funds we spent in refurbishing the VA property.

We advised the VA that our lease had 15 more years until expiration in December 2024. We believed that our continuing viability was in jeopardy.

We sent a formal letter to the Department of Veterans Affairs, dated September 9, 2009 in which we proposed contract changes or a termination settlement.

Proposed Contract Changes or Termination Settlement

Option A

1. Amend the contract to allow service of alcohol (i) inside the theatres at all events subject only to approved security conditions, (ii) at events on the grounds in enclosed tents subject to security conditions as applied between 2001-2007.

2. Extend the amended contract for a term not less than 30 years from the date of the amendment.

3. Compensation for demonstrated lost revenue due to the event rejections between August 2007 and the date of the amendment.

4. Mechanism to allow for accelerated recovery of invested capital improvements, plus remobilization costs at a rate of return to be agreed upon and guaranteed.

5. Granting WADSWORTH THEATRE MANGEMENT additional revenue opportunities, including the right to manage all movie shoots on DVA property, as well as the right to manage and collect all parking concessions on DVA property, and any and all similar revenue streams.

Option B

If the parties are unable to agree on contract changes that meet their respective needs, then the contract should be terminated by mutual agreement. The elements that the WADSWORTH THEATRE

MANAGEMENT would need in any termination agreement would include the following:

1. A guaranteed lump sum reimbursement for WTM's capital improvements on the property, with an agreed upon rate of return;

2. Compensation for demonstrated lost revenue due to the event rejections between August 2007 and the date of termination.

3. A procedure to determine WTM's entitlement to compensation for lost profits from the date of the termination. Agreement to the current date of the expiration, December 31, 2025, and full payment of all sums within 90 days of the date of the Termination agreement;

4. All other allowable costs as permitted by applicable law.

The VA did not accept any of our options. We then proceeded to get an attorney to represent us as we were getting nowhere toward making a settlement.

After many months of negotiating and with the help of our attorneys, on Sept. 23, 2010, we entered into a settlement agreement to terminate our lease, or as they referred to it, their "Enhanced Health Care Resources Sharing Agreement."

In spite of the fact that we received several million dollars as a settlement, I personally had mixed emotions. I enjoyed having an operation in Los Angeles and providing entertainment to the public there. But it was just an example of that old saying, "Always expect the unexpected."

Part V
The Final Curtain

Chapter 42
The Sale of the Helen Hayes Theatre – The Saga Begins

Over the years, almost on a monthly basis, I received calls asking if I were interested in selling the Helen Hayes. My answer was always, "No. Not interested." These calls came from producers, real estate brokers, and representatives of outside interests claiming to have clients looking to purchase a theatre on Broadway. The would-be buyers were from the U.S., London, Japan, Korea, China and elsewhere. They included many "wannabes" hoping to get into the theatre business and many producers who wanted to own their own theatre.

In the spring of 2008, I received a call from Ellen Richards, who at the time was the Executive Director of Second Stage Theatre, an off-Broadway, non-profit theatre. They were renting a 296-seat theatre but were looking to move to Broadway and wanted to buy the Helen Hayes.

I knew of their theatre as I had seen many plays there and knew the quality of their work – especially their contemporary American plays. I felt the Hayes would be a perfect fit for them. They'd also be eligible for Tony Award consideration. Nevertheless, I told her the theatre was not for sale at that time.

Ellen then said, "If you were to sell it – throw out a price." I thought for a moment and then answered, "If I were to sell, it would be for no less than 25 million and that does not include air rights, which we would retain."

After several weeks, I again received a call from Ellen Richards, this time telling me that they were prepared to pay the $25,000,000 exclusive of the air rights. I was stunned at the offer and told her that I would think about it and discuss it with my partner, Jeff Tick (son of my, late long-time partner, Donald Tick) and the Tick Family.

Why Sell Now? After the conversation with Ellen, I started to reflect on the reality of our situation. I have always had a knack for being able to anticipate what may be coming. So, I started to think about the changes coming to the theatre business and how they would affect the Hayes. Here are all the factors I weighed when considering the $25,000,000 offer for the theatre.

The Need for Star Power: To begin with, more and more producers were feeling that they needed to have a famous star or two to assure the success of their plays and musicals. And stars were only willing to give a limited commitment to a theatrical presentation – typically between six to eight weeks. Therefore, producers would need to be in theatres with a larger seating capacity so that they would have a chance to pay back their investors and make a profit while the star was in the show.

With only 600 seats and no possibility of adding more, the Hayes would not be able to remain competitive with the larger houses on Broadway. This, of course, would preclude the Hayes from ever getting top stars to perform at our theatre.

The Need for Further Renovations: At the same time, I was aware that our beloved theatre would be 100-years old in 2012. I foresaw a lot of expenses coming up with things breaking down. For one thing, the piping was as old as the building. For another, old buildings in New York were built with asbestos.

We were 'grandfathered' in when we purchased the theatre in 1979 and had never broken a wall with all our refurbishments. So, we never had to tackle that issue. But if we had to replace the pipes – or when we finally sold the building – either we or the new owners would have to comply with the rules of the day. Asbestos abatement alone would surely cost many millions of dollars and keep the theatre dark for well over a year, which is an extremely costly proposition for a tiny, single-theatre operation.

Increased Production Costs: I had also watched the cost of producing shows increase substantially over the years. When I began in the industry, it cost approximately $200,000 to produce a play. Then, even if we sold only 40% of the tickets for each show, we could still make a profit. This was no longer true.

Now, it costs about $3,000,000 to produce a play, which is a whole lot harder to raise and to recoup. Accounting for this 15-fold increase is the rise in the costs of salaries, sets, costumes, labor, insurance and real estate taxes.

These escalating costs meant that we would not be able to get big shows at the HHT because producers all wanted bigger theatres so they could sell more tickets to recover their costs and make a profit. This trend is certain to continue into the future, here again making our limited seating capacity a liability for us in ways it hadn't been before. This is what's happening in the theatre business today.

Rising Ticket Prices were another issue: When tickets were reasonably priced, theatre-going people would see 20-30 shows/year. Now they pick and choose because of the costs. Today $150 is the normal price so audiences want to be highly selective.

If $300-$400 becomes the norm, then it's $600-$800 a show for a couple. Today, people are spending $1500 and more to see Hamilton.

Again, I knew I couldn't charge such prices because I didn't have the stars. I also knew that the prices were going to continue to go up and union rates along with them. With only a limited number of seats to fill for every performance, the show would soon cost more than potential profits in our theatre.

Making the Hard Decision: Fortunately, I had the vision to see that it was the right price at the right time and the right thing to do. Thus, I took the offer from Second Stage to the Tick Family. They were very surprised at the amount offered. Nevertheless, Jeff Tick and his family were reluctant to sell the theatre. After many discussions, however, they saw the validity in my reasoning and agreed that, indeed, this might be the best time to sell and the best offer we would get.

Being part of an elite Broadway scene for so many years, and being recognized as an important part of the theatre industry, my emotions started to stir up doubts once again. Could I give up the prestige of being one of the few theatre owners on Broadway?

Even in the face of all these very good reasons to sell, it was still a tough decision. But I knew it was the right time, the right price, and the right buyer.

Why Sell to Second Stage? No other buyer could give us the kind of money Second Stage offered. They were able to do so because, as a nonprofit, they get their capital from donations. So, it's the public's money that buys their theatre. (The City of New York ultimately gave them $10,000,000 toward the renovations once they owned the theatre). Thus, we made the decision to sell to them.

A deal was signed with Second Stage in April 2008. They gave us a large, non-refundable deposit. A closing date was set that coincided with the closing of the show that was running at out theatre. We expected to close the sale in 2009.

Chapter 43
Bumps Along the Road – Lead to an Unexpected Windfall

Then, the stock market fell, and the recession of 2008 made fund-raising impossible. When it came time to close the sale, Second Stage did not have their funding and requested a one-year extension.

We granted the extension provided that we could book and operate the theatre to avoid being dark and without revenue to cover our high expenses. And if the new show was a hit, then Second Stage would have to agree that the sale closing would be postponed until the conclusion of the run of the show in the theatre. Second Stage agreed.

After that first year, there were several more extensions requested by Second Stage that we also granted since they were continuing to have difficulty raising the funds needed to close the sale.

Then, around Thanksgiving 2010, I received that fateful call from Nick Scandalios of the Nederlander Organization asking for a favor.

They had a big new show with a major star due to come in almost immediately; and they didn't have any place to put it.

Their new show would have a limited run and was guaranteed to sell out. The star was Robin Williams.

If you're not familiar with how Broadway operates, then you may well wonder how they could have booked such a big show without first making sure they had a large enough theatre to accommodate the audience. Actually, there's a very good reason for what might seem like a very backward approach.

To get Robin Williams in his heyday – and not lose out to the competition – a major theatre owner had to just go ahead and book it. And when you own nine theatres on Broadway, as the Nederlanders do, you are fairly confident that you will have one or two shows that will close at just the right time. Only this time, it didn't work out.

However, they had one show that wasn't filling all the seats. So, they needed to be able to move it to a smaller house and use the larger venue for Robin Williams. They thought that our then-current attraction would be closing shortly and asked if they could move a show from one of their theatres to the Helen Hayes.

The producers of the show that they were proposing to move were agreeable with the proposed switch since Nederlander was paying for a large portion of the move. They also felt that the Helen Hayes would be a perfect fit for them.

Rock of Ages, the show that Nick and the Nederlander Organization wanted me to take, was a big, loud rock'n roll show. It would be moving from the Brooks Atkinson on 47th St – a theatre with 100% more stage space and 45% more seats than the HHT. (1070 seats compared to our 600).

The lower operating costs at the Helen Hayes, plus the smaller scale, would be the perfect fit for this show. After all, they hadn't been selling out their much larger theatre. And as old adage on Broadway goes, 'The tougher it is to get a ticket, the more tickets you will sell.'

Since Second Stage was still not ready to close the sale, I was wondering whether I really wanted a rock show as I already had several other shows I was looking to book. I told Nick "I would love to do you a favor, but heavy 80's rock is not my choice for the Hayes." At this point they were desperate and suggested I have dinner with the producer and see the show.

My General Manager, Susan Myerberg, had already been in touch with the *Rock of Ages* management and was eager to make this show work at the Hayes. She also encouraged me to be open to the wild fun and commercial possibilities of the run. I agreed to have dinner with Susan and one of the show's producers and to see the show.

At dinner, I told the producer I would probably leave at intermission, as I don't enjoy rock'n roll. Much to my surprise, however, I did enjoy the show. I also watched all the happy faces on the people in the audience and saw how much they enjoyed this show. It was more like a rock audience than a traditional theatre audience. At intermission, I looked at Susan and the producer and told them I had decided to stay till the end.

At the end of the show, I again experienced the wild enthusiasm of the audience and said, "This could work for us." Susan agreed, and we booked the show. The director and designers got busy reducing the scenery and revising the action so that our theatre was indeed the perfect fit.

I was sure the show would not last for more than several months. It had already played off-Broadway at New World Stages and then on Broadway at the Brooks. It was not selling out and did not attract the Broadway theatre crowd.

I was in excellent company in my belief that this show would not last until our new closing date for the sale to Second Stage, which at that point was May 2012. The traditional Broadway thought was against the show running for any extended period of time. So, I suggested to my staff that we start looking for a backup.

Much to my surprise, however – and the shock of the Broadway industry – *Rock of Ages* was a giant success at the Hayes. We opened in March 2011 and ran almost four years, closing in January 2015. This show turned out to be my longest running and most profitable show at our theatre in the 37 years that we owned it.

Chapter 44
The Helen Hayes Theatre
Centennial Celebration

It was early in the year 2012 and it looked like *Rock of Ages* was still going strong. Therefore, the sale to Second Stage would not happen for a while.

Our House Manager, my nephew, Alan Markinson, was our resident theatre historian. He had spent many hours in the New York Public Libraries and also at The Shubert Archive, where the Shubert Organization collects and houses the records of the Broadway theatres, studying our theatre's history and copying old photos for our own archives. He very much wanted to celebrate the 100th birthday of our beloved theatre.

Alan presented a solid plan to celebrate the historic occasion. It included inviting members of the industry – with a special emphasis on all who had worked on an attraction at the theatre over the many years. He also wanted to use this lovely anniversary party as our farewell since the sale would happen at the conclusion of the *Rock of Ages* run – whenever that took place.

I agreed that a party would be a great idea. After owning and operating the theatre for approximately 37 years, I was very emotionally tied to it. So what better way for me to draw the curtain on that fabulous period in my life than having a big party?

Alan, along with Susan Myerberg, our General Manager, got busy retaining the services of a theatre press agent as well as photographers and videographers. The celebratory show on our stage would be produced by one of our former administrators, Carla Weiss, and we were overjoyed when Harvey Fierstein agreed to emcee the show!

We contacted the actors who had performed at the theatre in various plays and musicals over the years and asked if they would make a presentation on stage. We wanted them to talk about their experiences at the theatre or perform an excerpt of a show they had been in at the HHT. Then afterwards we would invite the attendees to a large afternoon party at Sardi's.

The turnout for the show was tremendous – the theatre was completely full. The party afterwards was also fabulous with a constant flow of people coming and going.

The theatre business is a small community so this was a wonderful opportunity to see some people for the first time in years and to enjoy reminiscing with them.

Many people came over to me at the party to talk about their experiences at the Helen Hayes and all the fun and excitement they'd had. One old-time box office treasurer, now retired, reminded me of the time we were both in the box office at intermission on a Wednesday matinee when an older gray-haired woman, perhaps in her 80s, came to the box office and said, "I am a very religious, church-going person who never uses profanity. This show uses so much terrible profanity that I can no longer go back in and watch the rest of the show. I would like to have my money back."

The treasurer looked at this sweet old lady and said, "I'm sorry you didn't enjoy the show, but I can't give you a refund.[4]" She looked him straight in his eyes and said, "If you're not going to give me a refund then GO FUCK YOURSELF!" And walked out.

I was also reminded by an usher who was with us for many years

---

[4] In the theatre world, once you buy a ticket it's yours. All sales are final. Otherwise, we'd have madness!

that when I produced and brought *Torch Song Trilogy* and Harvey Fierstein to the theatre, that Harvey was very superstitious as many actors are. He insisted on keeping his pet rabbit in his dressing room at all times. He felt it was his good luck charm and he was not about to give it up. Since he was both the author and the star of the show, I allowed it.

As you know, the show was a hit and ran for three years. Harvey stayed in the show for one year, and so did the rabbit - and so did the odor. I, for one, can honestly say that Harvey's rabbit had the longest theatre run of any rabbit in the theatre business.

For me, the day of the centennial will always be imbedded in my memory. It was a wonderful way to say goodbye to a beautiful theatre.

The following pages include some of the special materials created for the Centennial Celebration.

THE LITTLE / HELEN HAYES THEATRE
100 YEARS ON BROADWAY

1912-2012

THE LITTLE / HELEN HAYES THEATRE
I OO YEARS ON BROADWAY

Thursday, May 24, 2012

"Mere longevity is a good thing for those who watch life from the sidelines. For those who play the game, an hour may be a year, a single day's work an achievement for eternity." - Helen Hayes

Dear Friends,

We are so proud to celebrate the Little/Helen Hayes Theatre Centennial with you today. When we purchased this beautiful theatre in 1979, we counted on an amazing adventure as we emerged from the sidelines to play this game. For us, the years have felt like hours and each performance on our stage an eternal achievement.

We are delighted that our adventure includes our extended family – three generations in some cases – working tirelessly with talent, passion, ingenuity and loyalty, whether front of house, backstage or in the management office. In addition, every producer, writer, actor, director, choreographer, musician, designer, stage manager, technician and other company member who has called the Helen Hayes home will always be part of our family. *Rock of Ages* is the 44th production to open here since our purchase in 1979.

As the theater constantly teaches us, we open, we close and we keep on going. We mourn the passing of co-owner Donald Tick and are deeply grateful to the rest of our Helen Hayes family for continuing the tradition.

We are thrilled that the City of New York has marked the Little/Helen Hayes Theatre Centennial with a mayoral proclamation and are incredibly happy to share this wonderful day with all of you.

Welcome to our house. We hope you enjoy meeting and reconnecting with our family.

Warmest and Best Regards,

Martin Markinson and Jeffrey Tick

"The good die young, but not always. The wicked prevail, but not consistently...I feel safe within the confines of the theatre." - Helen Hayes

HELEN HAYES THEATRE CENTENNIAL CELEBRATION

Introduction:
Martin Markinson & Jeffrey Tick, Theatre Owners

Our Host:
Harvey Fierstein

 Harvey Fierstein is a four-time Tony Award winning writer and actor. He made his Broadway debut at this theatre starring in his celebrated play *Torch Song Trilogy* (1982-1985), for which he won two Tony Awards (Best Actor and Best Play), two Drama Desk Awards, a special Obie, a Theatre World Award and a Dramatists Guild Award. Rehearsals are currently underway in London for *Torch Song Trilogy*'s first major revival. His Broadway and screen writing credits also include *La Cage Aux Folles* (the only show to ever win Best Musical and 2 Best Revival Tony Awards), *Safe Sex* (Ace Award),*Legs Diamond, A Catered Affair* (12 Drama Desk nominations and the Drama League Award for Best Musical) and *Newsies The Musical*, which is now playing at the Nederlander Theatre and recently earned 8 Tony nominations including Best Musical and Best Book of a Musical for Mr. Fierstein. Other plays include *Spookhouse, Forget Him* and *Flatbush Tosca*. He has also appeared on the Broadway stage as an actor in *Safe Sex, Hairspray* (Tony, Outer Critics Circle and the Drama League Award for Outstanding Performer of the Year), *Fiddler on the Roof* (also on tour), *A Catered Affair* and, most recently, *La Cage aux Folles*. His teleplays include *Tidy Endings* for HBO (ACE Award), and *On Common Ground* for Showtime. His children's HBO special, *The Sissy Duckling*, won the Humanitas Prize and the book version is in its fifth printing. He has also won a NY Magazine Award, and nominations for The Olivier Award and an Emmy. His political writings have been seen on PBS' series "In The Life" and published in *The NY Times, Huffington Post* and *Hartford Courant*. He was inducted into The Theater Hall of Fame in 2008 and is currently collaborating on the musical *Kinky Boots* with Cyndi Lauper. His political editorials have been published in *The New York Times, TV Guide*, The Huffington Post, and broadcast on PBS's *In the Life*. He is known worldwide for his performances in films like *Mrs. Doubtfire* and *Independence Day*, and television shows such as "How I Met Your Mother," "American Family," "Cheers" (Emmy nomination), "The Simpsons," and "Nurse Jackie."

Special Appearances by Helen Hayes Theatre Alumni from shows* including:

*Subject to change

Please join us next door at **Sardi's Restaurant** for a special reception immediately following this event.

Reprinted from special Helen Hayes Theatre Centennial
Celebration *Playbill*. Used with permission. Playbill, Inc. New York
City, Philip Birsh, President & CEO. All rights reserved.

Martin Markinson and Jeffrey Tick holding
the Mayor Bloomberg Proclamation
Photograph ©2012 Lyn Hughes. Photo by Lyn Hughes.

The text of Mayor Bloomberg's Proclamation follows.

PROCLAMATION

I, MICHAEL R. BLOOMBERG, MAYOR OF THE CITY OF NEW YORK, IN RECOGNITION OF THIS IMPORTANT EVENT, DO HEREBY PROCLAIM THURSDAY, MAY 24, 2012, IN THE CITY OF NEW YORK AS "HELEN HAYES THEATRE DAY."

"Theatre and the performing arts have always been an integral part of life in New York. The bright lights of Broadway continue to draw thousands of tourists to our City, and the musicals, plays, and concerts that take place here every day are vitally important to New York's economic success and international cultural leadership. The work of our thriving theatrical community has helped our city remain a leader in the field, and we're pleased to join in celebrating the centennial anniversary of one of Broadway's most long-standing and distinctive venues—the Helen Hayes Theatre.

"In an industry known for being big, bold, and brash, the intimacy of the 590-seat Helen Hayes Theatre is something that audiences continue to seek out. As the smallest of Broadway's 40 professional theatres, it proves that size doesn't matter when it comes to success. Since its 1912 opening run of John Galsworthy's *The Pigeon*, the theatre has gone on to serve as the home of television programs like *The Dick Clark Show* and now hosts contemporary stage hits like *Rock of Ages, The 39 Steps*, and *Xanadu*. Designated as a landmark by the Landmarks Preservation Commission in1987, the Helen Hayes Theatre has truly earned its place in Broadway history.

"Under the ownership of Martin Markinson and the Tick family, and with the guidance of the Little Theatre Group LLC, the Helen Hayes Theatre has become one of the most distinguished stages of Broadway. This event gives all of us the opportunity to recognize a true New York institution, and to reflect on the important role that the performing arts play in making all parts of our city great. Together, we can look forward to another hundred and more years of achievement, innovation, and excellence along the Great White Way."[54]

---

[5] As antiquated and offensive as this term may sound to contemporary audiences, it has an interesting and innocent origin. In the pre-20th Century theatre world, fires were a regular hazard because of the dangers of gas lighting in poorly ventilated theatres. With Edison's invention of the electric light bulb, theatres were safely illumined and marquees along Broadway were lit up with bright, dazzling signage. Hence, Broadway became known as 'The Great White Way.' This was described in colorful language by the journalist Will Irwin in 1927: "Mildly insane by day, the square goes divinely mad by night. For then on every wall, above every cornice, in every nook and cranny, blossom and dance the electric advertising signs ... All other American cities imitate them, but none gets this massed effect of tremendous jazz interpreted in light." [Source: Spotlightonbroadway.com]

Selected Photographs from the Centennial Celebration[6]

Mandy Patinkin

Harvey Fierstein, Host; with Martin Markinson,
Jeffrey Tick, speakers, performers and staff

Steve Guttenberg and Martin Markinson

Tony Roberts

Party at Sardi's

Martin Markinson and Harvey Fierstein

Chapter 45
The Sale of the Helen Hayes Theatre – The Saga Concludes

In November 2014, when the *Rock of Ages* producers informed us that they would be closing in January 2015, we immediately notified Second Stage that the theatre sale would close in February 2015, ninety days after the show vacated the theatre, in accordance with the original 2008 Second Stage sale agreement. However, Second Stage's financing was still incomplete and they requested a further extension to close the sale.

In the original 2008 sales agreement, extensions to the closing date could be agreed upon – provided that Second Stage covered the cost of our theatre sitting dark. Or, in the alternative, we would book an interim show to cover the costs. This had been the procedure we followed during the entire period from 2008 through all of Second Stage's requested and granted extensions to the closing date.

However, to my amazement and shock – especially given the good and cordial relationship we had enjoyed with Second Stage during all of these years – they said that they would not approve another booking while they finished their capitalization, nor would they pay our expenses to stay dark. Then, they filed a lawsuit in the NY State Supreme Court to get a "free" extension.

What a terrible waste of time and money! We were defending ourselves in court by simply pointing to the original 2008 contractual provisions that controlled this situation.

Thankfully, the judge agreed with us and told Second Stage, in essence, 'You don't go to a closing with a commitment, you go with cash. I'll give you an extension but that's the last one and you'll pay for that extension.' Second Stage was given the time to conclude their financing – providing they would cover our costs to stay dark in the interim as originally agreed.

My partner was furious with Second Stage for putting us through this process. But I remained friendly with the artistic director and did my best to smooth things over.

The Tick Family actually offered to cancel the sale contract and return all of Second Stage's money if Second Stage could not raise the funds. In addition, Jeff Tick introduced Second Stage to our extremely capable bankers at Signature Bank.

Second Stage declined the offer to cancel the contract. They then used Signature's services and put together the complex financial transaction to close the sale – finally – in April of 2015.

Once the sale was complete, I again had mixed emotions about no longer being a theatre owner on Broadway. There was the sadness I felt at the loss of belonging to such an elite group. I believed my importance in the industry would fade and I wondered how I would deal with this emotionally.

However, as you shortly will read, I continued to be a producer on Broadway for a short while afterwards. And this diminished my sadness since I still remained involved in the business I'd loved so fully for so long.

SECOND STAGE'S POINT OF VIEW

On August 19, 2016, I came across an article written by Philip Boroff in Broadway Journal (broadwayjournal.com) that reflects Mr. Boroff's reporting on the financial, artistic and other aspects of the sale. I find it interesting to understand a different point of view, and so, with generous permission from and special thanks to Philip Boroff and Broadway Journal (broadwayjournal.com), the article in its entirety follows. (©2016 Philip Boroff. All rights reserved.)

SECOND STAGE BORROWED $16.5 MILLION FOR HELEN HAYES, BACKED BY PROSPECTIVE 'FROZEN' LANDLORD

August 19, 2016 by Philip Boroff

Proposed Facade of Helen Hayes/Rockwell Group via Landmarks Preservation Commission

EXCLUSIVE: Second Stage Theatre has less than two years to repay a $16.5 million mortgage on its new Broadway home.

In April 2015, the nonprofit completed its long-awaited purchase of the Helen Hayes Theatre. The "amazing moment," as Artistic Director Carole Rothman

put it, should help raise the profile of the 37-year-old company and the
contemporary American plays and musicals it produces, which have
won three Pulitzer Prizes since 2010. But in buying Broadway's smallest
venue, Second Stage accepted a big burden.

The $16.5 million loan from Signature Bank matures in April 2017. It can be
extended for just 12 months, according to Second Stage's most
recent financial statement. A person briefed on the fundraising said it
still seeks a multi-million-dollar donor who'd have the option to rename the
Helen Hayes. Second Stage is also offering naming rights for the theater's six
bathrooms, five dressing rooms, two lounges, two offices and the lobby, bar
and elevator. A spokesman declined to comment.

The short maturity of the loan — for two-thirds of the $25 million purchase —
suggests that Rothman and Executive Director Casey Reitz believe they can
raise funds fast, notwithstanding their past struggles. The
pressure won't disappear: Second Stage has said it plans to double its annual
budget — now $8 million. For a nonprofit on Broadway — i.e. the
Roundabout, Lincoln Center Theater, Manhattan Theatre Club and now
Second Stage — "the fundraising is even more crucial on an ongoing basis,"
said Steven Chaikelson, head of Columbia University's theater management
and producing concentration. When ticket sales fall short of internal
projections, an organization must compensate with increased contributions
or future sales, he said. (As at other nonprofits, Second Stage gets help with
expenses on some shows from commercial producers, such as with the
musicals *Dear Evan Hansen* and *Next to Normal*.)

The company originally sought to buy its 296-seat off-Broadway rental on
West 43rd St.; the landlord wanted a "phenomenal" sum, recalled Ellen
Richard, Second Stage's executive director from 2006 to 2009. A deal for the
597-seat Hayes was signed in April 2008, but fundraising was promptly
suspended amid the financial crisis. Twice Second Stage postponed the
closing, originally set for June 2010. Then it was tabled during the

commercial run of the musical *Rock of Ages* in the Hayes. After *Rock of Ages* shuttered, Second Stage sued the seller — Martin Markinson and Jeffrey Tick — to gain more time. Rothman said in court papers that it couldn't secure financing without a closing date. Second Stage was granted a two-month, court-ordered extension, which added about $250,000 to the $24.75 million price. It completed the purchase through a limited liability corporation it created.

The Little Theatre, circa 1912

It received help from a rich neighbor. Jujamcyn Theatres, which owns five Broadway houses, agreed to provide Signature Bank with extra collateral for the Helen Hayes mortgage, according to property records. And Second Stage agreed to sell Jujamcyn an alleyway underneath an annex west of the Hayes, so Jujamcyn can expand the stage in the adjacent St. James Theatre. Jujamcyn paid Second Stage $5 million. The agreement will allow Jujamcyn to book more elaborate musicals in the St. James, such as *Frozen*, which is headed there in 2018, a person familiar with the landlord said. Jujamcyn President Jordan Roth declined to comment.

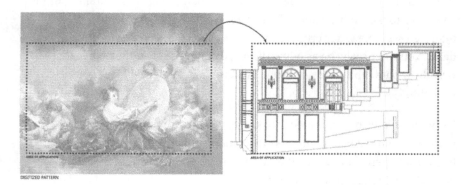

Rendering of digitized pattern applied to auditorium wall/Landmarks Preservation Commission

Being on Broadway should help Second Stage attract more stars, who can compete for Tony Awards. And ownership confers stability. "I don't know of any successful not-for-profit that doesn't have a permanent home," Ellen Richard said. She noted that an earlier employer of hers, the Roundabout, left its Times Square venue in 1999 under threat of eviction. "We had two theaters at the Criterion Center and it became a Toys 'R Us," said Richard, now interim executive director of the Laguna Playhouse.

New York City is beset with competing capital projects, including MCC Theater's new home on West 52nd Street. And foundations, which bless projects with their largesse and imprimatur, are cautious about investing in bricks and mortar for culture. "The sector nationally is overbuilt," said Sandi Clement McKinley, a vice president of the Nonprofit Finance Fund, which provides financing and consulting to nonprofits. "They want to do no harm. They're asking, 'is the organization able to take on the facilities and still pay day-to-day costs?'" (Even without the Hayes, Second Stage has struggled with its model, like the rest of the industry. Subscriptions, a top revenue source, declined in each of the past seven seasons, from $1.6 million in 2007-8 to $953,000 in 2014-15.)

Rothman, Second Stage's co-founder, expressed her own ambivalence about Broadway a decade ago. "I think you have to change your programming when you move to a Broadway house," she said in a November 2006 video interview with Newsday critic Linda Winer, just over a year before the Hayes deal. "You can't really be as adventurous, or I haven't seen the people that do Broadway shows be as adventurous. And you can't take as many risks, probably."

Yet with Broadway dominated by tourists who favor musicals, it could use more of Second Stage's contemporary American plays. The house that opened in 1912 as the Little Theatre is scheduled to reopen in 2017-18 following renovations overseen by the Rockwell Group, the firm led

by architect and Tony-winning scenic designer David Rockwell. The
project includes a new LED marquee, a restored interior and digitized images
on the walls based on tapestries that hung a century ago in the auditorium.
Second Stage has pledges, verbal and written, for the entire $22 million it
estimates the work will cost, including $10.5 million from the City of New
York, it said in the financial statement.

For the mortgage, all it needs is a rich person or entity looking to make a
mark on Broadway.

Chapter 46
What on Earth
Are Air Rights?

"Air Rights" is the name given to unused development rights that exist in the space above or around a building (literally in the air) on a real estate parcel,

For example, if the particular zoning laws permit a building of forty stories, and an existing building ¾ subject to those zoning laws ¾ is only four stories high, the land owner of that lot typically still has development rights to build an additional 36 stories above the four stories. Or, in certain special zoning areas and circumstances, the landowner may have the right to sell these unused development rights ("air rights") to the owner of an adjacent real estate lot.

The Helen Hayes Theatre, though the smallest of the Broadway theatres, had very valuable unused development rights (or unused "Air Rights") by virtue of being a landmarked building. This meant that we were prohibited by law from ever using these development rights above the theatre itself.

We had a total of 59,378 available square feet of development rights that we could not make use of at the HHT. But we could sell them. Unfortunately, the owners of the lots and buildings adjacent to ours did not want – or could not make use of – our air rights. This left us with no one to sell to under the "adjacent property" zoning laws.

However, when the Broadway theatres were landmarked, the theatre owners pressed the city for compensation, since we were precluded from responding to the future financial realities in the NYC real estate industry. We weren't allowed to tear down our buildings, turn them into other types of facilities, or build around them to create other structures that might hide or change the original landmarked theatre.

In the 1980s, the Shubert Organization, the largest of the Broadway theatre organizations and owner of the most Broadway theatres, sued the city for compensation and won.

The City, the Zoning Board, the City Planning office, and the Land Use Commission agreed to allow the owners of landmarked theatres to "float" their unused air rights to non-adjacent building sites. This meant that landmarked theatres could sell these extremely valuable development rights to one or more "receiving" sites within a specified midtown zoning area – 40th Street to 58th Street, 6th Avenue to 8th Avenue.[7]

A qualified developer under the zoning laws could purchase from the landmarked Broadway theatre owner the available air rights to allow that developer to build "extra" floors in their proposed buildings in excess of what the zoning for that lot would otherwise allow.

When these new zoning laws were passed – back in the 80s – I immediately got a call from a developer wanting to buy all of my available air rights for one million dollars.

My partner, Donald Tick, and I had the feeling that if we waited, the value of the air rights would only increase. I saw that the development within the theatre district was growing very fast, as developers were buying and demolishing small three and four-story buildings to build high-rise office buildings and condominiums.

After many ups and downs over the intervening years, my partner

---

[7] Remember that the Broadway theatre district runs from 41st to 54th Street, between Sixth and Eight Avenues – with Lincoln Center and Times Square also included.

Jeff Tick took this bull by the horns and became an expert in negoti-ating the sale of air rights. In 2015, Jeff negotiated two very lucrative deals for us with the owners of two separate eligible receiving sites.

So in 2016, after the contracts – and the complex, related filings – wound their way through the lawyers and the Landmarks and Land Use Commissions, we were able to sell air rights to two different developers in two separate transactions. Each transaction involved the "floating" of air rights from the Helen Hayes Theatre lot to their respective qualified receiving sites. We finally closed our air rights sales with both developers on February 3, 2016.

While each transaction is subject to confidentiality provisions, it can be disclosed that we sold 16,000 square feet to the owners of the site at 250 West 49th Street (between Broadway and 8th Avenue) and sold 41,355 square feet to the owners of the site at 1710 Broadway (a large, assembled parcel of four lots extending from 54th to 55th Streets and between 7th and 8th Avenues). The balance went to Second Stage Theatre as part of the building sale.

The total selling price was far in excess of the one million dollars offered many years prior. In fact, these rights sold for a little more than the theatre itself – $27,000,000! It was almost like winning the lottery.

At that point, every owner but the Shuberts had sold all of their air rights. The Shuberts had sold some but retained a significant amount of their air rights.

Chapter 47
Loyalty and Devotion

My immediate and full-time staff at the theatre consisted of only three people. **Susan Myerberg, General Manager
and General Counsel**, led our permanent staff.

Susan was my theatrical attorney for the show I produced in 1981,
Ned and Jack. A few years later, during the run of *Torch Song Trilogy* she
advised me that she was taking a sabbatical to attend Yale School of
Drama as a special student in theatre management and production
for the year. A month after she finished the program, she was working
at the Williamstown Theatre Festival – where I found her by phone.

I had just let go of the General Manager I worked with from the
time I bought the theatre, and asked Susan if she would like to take
that position at the Helen Hayes. She was thrilled and stayed with me
for thirty-five years as both General Manager and General Counsel.
During this time, Susan also worked on my other projects as well as
her own law practice and ventures, and co-produced the original
Driving Miss Daisy.

Alan Markinson, House Manager, is my nephew. At the age
of twenty he left his home in Florida, came to New York to try to
find work in any capacity he could in the theatre world. He worked

at various jobs both in and outside of the theatre industry for about two years until an opportunity arose at my newly acquired Little Theatre. My house manager had retired, and I offered that job to Alan. He was with me at the theatre for thirty-four years. However, he took occasional leaves of absence to company manage Broadway and touring shows.

Hector Angulo, House Engineer: Hector and his uncle, Juan, were working for Westinghouse when it owned the theatre. They knew every inch of the building and whatever was needed to operate the theatre. I hired them immediately and when Juan left, Hector became the sole house engineer. The Hayes was Hector's home and he maintained it to the utmost of his ability, which helped us become an efficiently operating theatre. He worked with his wife and two children on staff when needed. He was with me for thirty-seven years.

Susan, Alan, Hector and his family were all integral and beloved members of our Helen Hayes family. Over the years, they could have worked with larger theatre organizations and possibly made more money. Hector was constantly receiving invitations to work elsewhere for more. But we all stayed together, and they helped make our theatre the success that it was. I was truly blessed to receive such loyalty and devotion from them. I am deeply grateful to them all.

<u>All Hands On Deck</u>: When a show was running, we needed many more people to help make it successful. These included stagehands, box office treasurers, ticket takers, ushers and various others. The stagehands and treasurers were members of various unions that had multi-year contracts with our theatre.

As previously described, when we booked a show, we would hire these union members for the run of the attraction, as well as our non-union front of house team. When the show closed, they would take jobs at other theatres or elsewhere until we rebooked. Once we did, then they would usually return to work with us at the Helen Hayes. We could not have accomplished all that we did without our union and non-union staff. We deeply appreciate the many years of loyal service we received from such talented and dedicated people who helped to make our theatre such a shining success on Broadway.

Martin Markinson, Alan Markinson, Susan
Myerberg, Jeff Tick, Hector Angulo
Photograph ©2012 Lyn Hughes. Photo by Lyn Hughes.

Chapter 48
Back to Producing

I found a musical I was excited about that was being put together by a friend of mine. It was called *Honeymoon in Vegas,* and in August 2013, I became part of the producing group.

This was originally a 1992 Hollywood movie, written and directed by Andrew Bergman without a musical score. The idea was that Bergman would write the book for the musical, add music and lyrics by Jason Robert Brown, and bring it to Broadway. We were able to get the movie, television, and stage actor Tony Danza to try the show out of town to see how it went. This would allow us to make improvements before bringing it to Broadway.

We opened in October 2013 at the Paper Mill Playhouse in New Jersey and not only did we get very good reviews overall, the *New York Times* review was a rave.

Every time I saw the show, I was impressed by the audience's reaction. There was always a standing ovation at the curtain call. The show needed very few changes and we all felt we had a winner on the way to Broadway.

We opened at the Nederlander Theatre on January 15, 2015. But despite the almost unanimous good reviews and the wonderful audience reaction, we were unable to keep the show running and were forced to close on March 30, 2015.

This particular show was a big disappointment for me, as I believed it had all the ingredients to become a big hit. However, as Oscar-winning playwright William Goldman once said, "Broadway is a high-risk business." This is certainly true. However, I've always believed that if you are afraid of failing, you will never try. And if you never try, you can never succeed.

Next, since I was looking for another musical, I joined the producing team that was doing the revival of *Gigi*. The show went into rehearsal on December 8, 2014 and played at the John F. Kennedy Center for the Performing Arts in Washington D.C. from January 16 to February 12, prior to opening on Broadway in 2015.

Gigi already had quite a history. It originated as a 1945 novella by the French novelist Colette. It was then adapted for the screen and starred Danièle Delorme in the title role in 1948. Then, in 1951 Anita Loos adapted the novel for the stage and the Broadway production of *Gigi* catapulted a newcomer, Audrey Hepburn, to international stardom. She was quickly snapped up by Paramount Pictures to play the Princess in the movie, *Roman Holiday*, which won her an Oscar for Best Actress.

MGM secured the rights to the play and, in 1958, turned it into a movie musical with music written by Alan Jay Lerner and Frederick Loewe – fresh off their Broadway success with *My Fair Lady*. The movie starred Leslie Caron, Louis Jourdan, and Maurice Chevalier. It won nine Oscars – including Best Picture – plus three Golden Globe Awards. It also won a Grammy for Best Score. Then, in 1973, Lerner and Loewe adapted the movie for Broadway.

Our revival at the Kennedy Center, which was adapted by Heidi Thomas, received warm reviews but no raves. Nevertheless, the audience appeared to enjoy the show and almost every performance was sold out.

I found it to be a fun show with a wonderful musical score. The starring role of Gigi was performed by a young actress named Vanessa Hudgens, who rose to fame on Disney Channel's *High School Musical*.

We moved it from Washington D.C. to Broadway and, after running for several months, we were given a spot to perform a musical number from the show at the Tony Awards ceremony. We continued to run until the end of June and closed after a total run of approximately six months.

Producers are often asked, "Why did your show close so early?" Most of the producers I know usually have a pocket full of excuses to offer. As for me, my answer is always the same: "We simply didn't sell enough tickets." Why that is – is mostly a mystery.

Funding and producing a show can take one or two years of your life – sometimes even more. It is not an easy process. There are many ups and downs on the road to opening a show on Broadway – if you're lucky enough to get that far. Even then, it can be a hit or miss affair despite having all the right ingredients, as *Honeymoon in Vegas* and *Gigi* both demonstrated.

Now, on the verge of retirement, I wanted one last fling at bringing a winning musical to Broadway. I knew the producers who were doing *On Your Feet* about the life and music of the 26-time Grammy Award-winning husband-and-wife team Gloria and Emilio Estefan (with music and a book written by Alexander Dinelaris). It sounded like it had great potential to me. So I told the producers that I would like to be involved in some way and they were happy to have me on board.

The opening was on November 5, 2015 at the Marriott Marquis Theatre and was favorably received by the critics. The show ran for two years on Broadway, closed on August 20, 2017, and has been booked on a road tour in the US and internationally for years to come. After it was over, I was done.

I still get approached to produce another show now and then. However, I am too deep into retirement to do that again. Producing is a long and arduous process. And as much as I enjoyed it, I have taken my final bow in the wild world of show business.

In recalling my forty-year career in theatre, people ask me, and I have asked myself, if I have any regrets. And after giving it a great deal of thought I find I have only one regret: I didn't produce *Hamilton!*

ROB
McCLURE

BRYNN
O'MALLEY

AND

TONY DANZA

HONEYMOON
in VEGAS
THE MUSICAL

VICTORIA CLARK   COREY COTT   DEE HOTY   HOWARD McGILLIN

AND

VANESSA HUDGENS

Gigi

The Broadway Musical

Choose L'amour

ALSO STARRING STEFFANIE LEIGH

BOOK & LYRICS BY *Alan Jay Lerner*

MUSIC BY *Frederick Loewe*

A NEW BOOK ADAPTATION BY *Heidi Thomas*

CHOREOGRAPHED BY *Joshua Bergasse*

DIRECTED BY *Eric Schaeffer*

BASED ON THE NOVEL BY COLETTE

N NEIL SIMON THEATRE · GIGIONBROADWAY.COM

Her voice.
His vision.
Their story.
ON YOUR FEET!
THE STORY OF EMILIO & GLORIA ESTEFAN
MARQUIS THEATRE, 46TH ST. BETWEEN BROADWAY & 8TH AVE.
TICKETMASTER.COM 877-250-2929
OnYourFeetMusical.com

Part VI
Encore!

Epilogue: Give My Regards to Broadway

On February 24, 2018, *The New York Times* announced, "*Torch Song* is set to return to its original Broadway home, the Helen Hayes Theatre, on November 1, 2018. Moises Kaufman will direct the revised revival and Richie Jackson the lead producer said:

> 'Who couldn't use a dose of Harvey Fierstein right now? When you go to see one of his shows you know you're going to laugh, you know it's going to have an emotional impact and you know it's going to be about family. No matter what family you're a part of, you're going to see your family up there on the stage.'"

I felt a wonderful warmth and pride reading this. After 36 years it would be like turning back the clock for me to that amazing theatrical odyssey that culminated in the Tony Award and ended up having such a large positive impact on the lives of so many people. Thank you Harvey! You are back home for everyone to see and enjoy and laugh and cry – again!

Reflecting on my life – where I started and where I am now – it is clear to me that trusting my instincts, not looking back, and refusing to waste time on worry and regret have all combined to afford me a wonderful life and an amazing career on Broadway.

Much of my good fortune relates to good timing. For instance, when the Nederlanders needed a theatre for *Rock of Ages* so they could accommodate Robin Williams, we got our longest-running and most popular show to ever play at the Helen Hayes Theatre – with no production costs to us. And this occurred while we were waiting for Second Stage to secure their financing to buy us out.

Decades before that there was that day in the late '70s when I happened to be in New York and decided to drop in on my friend Ashton Springer, who had his office in the Little Theatre. Once I learned from Ashton that he was about to relocate because of the impending sale of the theatre, the wheels were set in motion that completely redirected the course of my life.

Largely thanks to that day, and all that followed from it, I've seen and heard so much. I had the opportunity to work with a lot of remarkable and talented individuals, many of whom were real characters from a vanishing era. I felt the indescribable sensation of hearing the name of the play I championed and produced be announced as the winner of that year's Tony awards. And I've had the disappointment of watching fine plays close too soon. I've watched the whimsical mind of the audience create unexpected Broadway miracles and flops.

Many producers seem to believe that they know the pulse of the public when they decide to produce a show for Broadway. I was never so presumptuous as to think I had the ability to judge what an audience would or would not like. I always took the approach that if I found a play or musical that was entertaining, provocative or funny to me – and I believed I could develop a good product – then I was willing to spend my time and money producing it. Doing this resulted in my hits as well as my flops.

It's important to mention, however, that as a theatre owner, and the operator of several theatres, it didn't always matter to me whether I liked a particular show if my theatres were dark. Sometimes, I would book a show out of necessity. Much to my surprise, some of these desperate-measure shows went on to become very successful and continued to run for quite a long time.

Through all these experiences, I've come to understand how much I love the theatre business and how lucky I am to have played the role that I did. This is a story I had to tell. My prayer is that it will be an enjoyable journey for the reader and a valuable legacy for those who are seeking to carve out a career on Broadway and are willing to face the inevitable ups and downs involved.

I have always felt a great deal of admiration for actors, singers and dancers – even more so after my own brief experience in front of the camera. The love and dedication of these performers to their profession – and their acceptance of the difficult competition they have to face each time they go out on auditions – is truly commendable to me.

When I lectured to the graduating theatre arts students that were planning to seek their future in the entertainment business, I always emphasized that they must be able to take a great deal of rejection and persevere in the face of it all. It's a very hard business but success is so sweet.

Every show I produced was like living a new adventure and I have done at least forty of them. I am often asked, "With the time and money involved in putting together a show, didn't you worry a lot?" So I share something that I read somewhere years ago: "Worrying is like sitting in a rocking chair. It gives you something to do but gets you nowhere." No, I have never really worried much. And this has kept me free to pursue what interested me.

The one thing I'm proudest of in my life is that with all of my success, it was never at anyone else's expense. I was considered a smart wheeler-dealer with a heart and a conscience. I enjoyed every day. And I am now enjoying retirement.

My wife, Arlena and I have been married for 56 years. Almost all of it was smooth sailing. However, there were times throughout the years when we encountered rough waters. Our love is a balancing act. We give and take, we fall and we catch one another. We are individuals and we are together. We may not always know the answers. We did not always make perfect decisions. But we always had and still have each other.

Arlena came to all of my openings, to the opening night parties, and to the backers' auditions with me. However, when I was in New York, I was working all day and going to shows every night, which wasn't really her 'thing.'

Over our many years together, while I've been involved in the entertainment industry, Arlena has been both a psychotherapist and a life coach. Today she is a nondenominational minister and has thus far performed over 600 weddings honoring Native American and Interfaith traditions. She is still going strong!

We now divide our time between Santa Fe, New Mexico and Maui, Hawaii. I also take occasional trips to New York to see Broadway shows for I am still a Tony voter.

Recently, Arlena and I sold our condo in Maui to purchase and remodel a beautiful house on the island. Our kids asked us, 'What are you guys doing?! People your age go in the opposite direction."

I told them that people our age know that they are living on borrowed time. And we want to make that time the happiest and most comfortable for ourselves as we possibly can. This is a whole new stage in our wonderful lives together, and we are enjoying it immensely.

Curtain Call: Some of the Secrets of Marty's Success

Editor's Note – These are the statements from Marty's unedited manuscript that caught my eye as I read through it for the first time. I organized and re-present them here because I felt they were useful to review and remember. Since Marty's life is such a beautiful illustration of the Law of Attraction – in action – I thought the reader might also enjoy this second glimpse into his life philosophy.

<u>Take a Leap of Faith</u>: After the purchase of the theatre, I decided to visit two prominent people in the theatre business. I went first to Jimmy Nederlander, whose organization owned nine theatres on Broadway. At our meeting, I told him I had just bought the Little Theatre and would greatly appreciate his advice on how I could learn about the way a theatre operates.

He didn't beat around the bush. "I believe you made a terrible mistake," he told me. "First of all, with only 500 seats, it's the smallest theatre on Broadway. It's a shit box and will never make any money. There's no way you can compete with me and other theatres owners to bring shows in. And when you don't have a show running, when the theatre is dark, you'll be losing a bundle."

I was so discouraged by these remarks that I was ready to shoot myself. But I reasoned that if I was going to shoot myself, I'd better do it in the foot so I'd still have my head to keep thinking about the mistake I might have just made.

Never one to be easily discouraged, however, I decided to talk to Bernie Jacobs, one of the heads of the huge Shubert Organization, which owned 17 of the 41 Broadway theatres. I sat down with him and repeated what I'd told Jimmy Nederlander. Bernie was a little kinder, but he still told me I was nuts.

I went home that evening and said to myself, 'What the heck do I do now? Since I only shot myself in the foot, I still have my brain. And dammit, I am going to make this thing work!' But how in the world could I compete? … I had to find a way!

Believe in Yourself: I learned to never get down on myself. Never to lose confidence. I taught myself not to let outside experiences affect the peace and calmness I wanted to feel. I believed if I learned how to handle disappointment, it would be easier to get on in life.

Luck Counts More Than Smarts: I still chuckle when I remember an old-time, very successful producer telling me at this time, "Every year you continue to produce on Broadway, you lose one point on your IQ." I thought about that and decided I would rather be lucky than smart. Actually, you've got to be a bit of both to succeed.

The Power of Synchronicity: I've had a very lucky life. And I always believe that in life, timing is very important. If you're lucky about the timing, certain things happen.

Go With Your Gut: "What the hell are you thinking?" I was asked. "A gay-themed show – never one like this on Broadway before. And it will run for four hours – it's crazy risky!" Again, I decided to go with my gut and take the risk. *Torch Song Trilogy* was not only a wonderful story; I felt it was a very important one to bring to a wide audience …

Generosity is a Wise Investment: Like life, the show was a process. For the first six months, it attracted primarily gay audiences. My partner Donald Tick and I put in our own money to keep it running. As the theatre owners, we were able to reduce the rent for the same reason.

Open Doors for Outsiders: Many people believe that this ground-breaking play, entering the mainstream on Broadway, provided an opening for gay people to come into their own with personal freedom and pride. It also inspired other producers of movies, TV and Broadway to take the leap and present gay-themed stories with gay actors.

Follow Your Heart: I once again went with my gut feeling and, regardless of my financial concerns, sold my interest in our insurance business to my partner. I was now 100% involved as a theatre owner and producer and was determined to succeed. I was now able to be fully engaged in the business I loved as both the owner of a theatre and the producer of shows in my theatre as well as in others.

Be Willing to Take Risks: I tell those people who ask, "Is producing for Broadway a form of gambling?" To some it is, for me, it's more of a creative endeavor that can bring joy and laughter, and stimulate an audience in ways that can have transformative and lasting effects. Win or lose, I feel that I have accomplished something magical, in addition to giving writers, actors, directors, designers, dancers and all the other theatrical people a chance to succeed and make a name for themselves.

Resolve Differences Rapidly: There can be many controversies when producing shows. I've never allowed disagreements to escalate. I resolved them quickly. Not being involved in any major disputes made my theatrical career very satisfying.

Pursue Your Passions: I stared at her. "Make a movie? What the hell do I know about making movies?" My wife laughed. "What the hell did you know about owning a theatre or producing shows on Broadway? And look at what you've accomplished!"

Cultivate Resilience in the Face of Disappointments: In spite of the fact that we received several million dollars as a settlement, I personally had mixed emotions. I enjoyed having an operation in Los Angeles and providing entertainment to the public there. But it was just one of those examples of that old saying, "Always expect the unexpected."

Learn to Read the Signs: I have always had a knack for being able to anticipate what may be coming.

Go for What You Want: As Oscar-winning playwright, William Goldman once said, "Broadway is a high-risk business." Nevertheless, I've always believed that if you are afraid of failing, you will never try. And if you never try, you can never succeed.

Forego Worry: Every show I produced was like living a new adventure and I have done at least 40 of them. I am often asked, "With the time and money involved in putting together a show, didn't you worry a lot?" I am then reminded of what I read somewhere: "Worrying is like sitting in a rocking chair. It gives you something to do, but it gets you nowhere." No, I have never really worried much, which kept me free to pursue what interested me.

A Simple, Reliable Formula: Reflecting on my life – where I started and where I am now – it is clear to me that trusting my instincts, not looking back, and refusing to waste time on worry and regret have all combined to afford me a wonderful life and an amazing career on Broadway.

Keeping Priorities Straight: I never dreamt of becoming wealthy or strived to become a millionaire. I had friends for whom having a lot of money was very important. It just was never that important to me. Only the lack of money.

Know the True Measure of Success: The one thing I am proudest of in my life is that with all of my success, it was never at anyone else's expense. … I was considered a smart wheeler-dealer with a heart and a conscience. And I enjoyed every day.

Chronology of Significant Dates and Events in Marty's History in Theatre

- 1975: Marty's 1st foray on Broadway: Invested and co-produced the musical, *Chicago*
- 1979: Purchased the Little Theatre in the Broadway District, next door to Sardi's
- 1982: Brought *Torch Song Trilogy* to the Little Theatre
- 1983: Won the Tony for Best Play with the *Torch Song Trilogy*
- 1983: Changed the name of the Little Theatre to the Helen Hayes Theatre
- 1989: Left the insurance business and became full-time in theatre
- 1998: Leased the Wadsworth Theatre – 1400 seats
- 2000-2006: Leased the Parker Theatre in Ft. Lauderdale – 1162 seats
- 2003: Leased the Brentwood Theatre – 500 seats
- 2008: A deal is signed to sell the Helen Hayes Theatre and the process commences
- 2011-2015: *Rock of Ages* at the Helen Hayes Theatre – ran for 2328 performances
- 2012: Centennial Celebration of the Helen Hayes Theatre
- 2015: Sale of the Helen Hayes Theatre to the Second Stage Theatre is completed
- 2015: Retirement commences

Appendices

What is Broadway?

Broadway is one of the biggest cultural attractions in New York – and in the world. Like London's West End theatre district, it is the place where what is considered to be the best commercial theatre in the English-speaking world is performed on stage and enjoyed by millions.

The Broadway District stretches between Sixth and Eight Avenues and from 41st to 54th Street. It started coming into being in the 1920s and '30's when a large number of the 41 commercial theatres in the area were built. There are older theatres there, as well – including the Helen Hayes, which opened in 1912.

The largest Broadway theatre is the Gershwin. Located at 222 West 51st St in New York, it seats 1935 people. The Helen Hayes Theatre, which is located at 240 West 44th St., is the smallest with a seating capacity of 595 people. The vast majority of the remaining 39 theatres have the capacity to seat well over 1000 patrons.

It is musical theatre that predominates on Broadway and helps set the tone for popular culture in the U.S. According to the Broadway League –

> "For the 2016–2017 season (which ended May 21, 2017), total attendance was 13,270,343 and Broadway shows had US $1,449,399,149 in grosses, with attendance down 0.4%, grosses up 5.5%, and playing weeks down 4.1%."[8]

---

[8] https://en.wikipedia.org/wiki/Broadway_theatre#cite_note-newleague-3

What is the Broadway League?

In 1930, the 'League of New York Theatres and Producers' was formed in an effort to combat the problem of ticket speculation and scalping. In its charter, the League specifies its purpose as –

> "…to protect the general public patrons of the theatre, owners of theatrical entertainments, operators of theatres and reputable theatre ticket brokers against the evils of speculation of theatre tickets."

By no means were they entirely successful in this venture. This is evidenced by the fact that Google recently instituted policies that force re-sellers to indicate that they are not directly affiliated with the venues. They also have to reveal their fees and mark-ups above the actual ticket price.[9]

Over time, the League of NY Theatres and Producers changed its name to the Broadway League. One of its primary roles is to negotiate contracts with the 14 labor unions. Their other missions include lobbying on behalf of theatre owners, working to develop audiences for the theatre, and running the annual Tony Awards to recognize excellence in all aspects of theatre.

---

[9] After standing by and watching ticket brokers buy up a bunch of tickets and then charge excessive rates for them, producers got smart and realized that they could do something similar. Now, when they have a highly popular show, they set aside several rows that offer the best view in the house and then sell them for more – as VIP seats. These are often the first seats to sell-out.

History of The Little Theatre
1912 - 1982

Whenever you go to a Broadway theatre, the complimentary copy of *Playbill* you receive will have the history of that particular theatre, including information on selected shows that played there. For theatre lovers who are also history buffs, this section is devoted to my theatre's history from its inception in the early 1900s through 1982 when we booked *Torch Song Trilogy*. The following pages are quoted from *Playbill's* archives, with very special thanks to – and extraordinary generous permission from – Playbill, Inc. NYC (© Playbill Inc. All rights reserved. Philip Birsh, President & CEO, Playbill, Inc.).

The Little Theatre was built by producer Winthrop Ames and opened on March 12, 1912. Ames, an aristocratic New Englander, rebelled against Broadway commercialism and built the Little Theatre, then with only 299 seats, as an intimate house for the production of non-commercial plays that were too risky to stage in large Broadway theatres. *The New York Times* admired the theatre's redbrick, green-shuttered exterior, its Colonial-style lobby with a fireplace, and the auditorium, which had no balcony or boxes and was built on an incline that afforded an unobstructed view of the stage.

The opening play was John Galsworthy's *The Pigeon*, which critic Ward Morehouse described as "a thoughtfully written comedy that brought forth human and delightful characterizations from Frank Reicher and Russ Whytal."

Ames's policy—to produce "the clever, the unusual drama that had a chance of becoming a library classic"—continued to be reflected in the Little Theatre's fare. Among the early productions, all financed solely by Ames, were George Bernard Shaw's *The Philanderer* (1913); *Prunella*, a fantasy by Laurence Housman and Harley Granville-Barker, starring Marguerite Clark and Ernest Glendinning (1913); and Cyril Harcourt's comedy, *A Pair of Stockings* (1914).

By 1915, Ames was having financial problems with 'The Little' as it was known for short. Because of his theatre's small seating capacity, the impresario was losing money, even with hits. On March 11, 1915, *The New York Times* reported that Ames was in danger of losing his house. To prevent this, Ames planned to increase the seating capacity to 1,000, add a balcony, and make the stage larger. In 1920, Burns Mantle reported that The Little had been remodeled and the seating capacity was now 450 seats.

Ames, whose money came from his family's manufacturing interests, began leasing The Little to outside producers, such as the highly respected John Golden and Oliver Morosco.

During the 1918-19 season, Rachel Crothers directed her own comedy, *A Little Journey*, at the Little. It ran for 252 performances. This was followed by another hit, *Please Get Married*, a farce starring Ernest Truex.

The true purpose of the Little Theatre, to present new playwrights and experimental dramas, was fulfilled by its next two bookings. In January 1920, Oliver Morosco presented *Mama's Affair*, a first play by Rachel Barton Butler that won a prize as the best drama written by a student of Professor George Baker's famous "English 47" class at Harvard. Morosco presented a cash reward to the author and mounted her play successfully, with Effie Shannon. The other drama was Eugene O'Neill's first full-length play, *Beyond the Horizon*, which had been playing matinees at other theatres before it was moved to the Little. It starred Richard Bennett and won the Pulitzer Prize.

The Little next housed one of its goldmines. *The First Year*, by actor Frank Craven, who starred in it with Roberta Arnold, proved to be a sensation. It opened on October 20, 1920, was produced by John Golden and ran for 760 performances. Producer Golden and playwright Craven thought that lightening might strike twice. In 1922, they tried again with Craven's *Spite Corner*, a small-town play about feuding families and lovers, but the comedy lasted only three months.

Guy Bolton, the prolific playwright who wrote many hit musicals and plays in his long career, had two comedies produced at the Little in 1923. The first, *Polly Preferred*, starring the vivacious blonde, Genevieve Tobin, and William Harrigan, was a daffy hit about a chorus girl who is sold to promoters like a product in a store window; the other, *Chicken Feed*, subtitled *Wages for Wives*, was really ahead of its time. It played just three years after women got the vote in the U.S. and would have delighted women's lib advocates a half-century later. As the title indicates, it was a comedic look at the unceasing labor of housewives and their paltry payment for it.

Ames continued to be the owner of the Little but it was leasing the theatre to producers like Golden, F. Ray Comstock and L. Lawrence Weber that made it viable for him. Weber was also managing the theatre.

However, as Brooks Atkinson reported in his book, *Broadway*, by 1922 Ames had lost $504,372 on the Little Theatre. His other theatre, The Booth, which he built with Lee Shubert in 1937, was a commercial house and is still successful today. When Ames died in 1937, his estate had dwindled to $77,000 and his widow was forced to move from the sprawling Ames mansion [located where?] to a small cottage on their estate.

In 1924, a play with the odd title, *Pigs*, turned out to be one of the year's best. Produced by John Golden, it starred Wallace Ford as a speculator who bought 50 sick pigs, cured them, and sold them at an enormous profit. He was greatly helped by his girlfriend, played by Nydia Westman who garnered love letters from the critics. The hit ran for 347 performances.

Thomas Mitchell proved popular in a 1926 comedy, *The Wisdom Tooth*, by Marc Connelly; *2 Girls Wanted* was a smash in 1926; *The Grand*

Street Follies, a popular annual revue that spoofed the season's plays and players, moved to The Little from the Neighborhood Playhouse in 1927; and Rachel Crothers returned to the Little with *Let Us Be Gay*, a 1929 hit, starring Francine Larrimore and Warren William.

In 1930, Edward G. Robinson was praised for his acting in both *Mr. Samuel*, and Elmer Rice's *The Left Bank* (1931), about Americans in Paris, which entertained patrons for 241 performances. A spate of plays with "Honeymoon" in their titles moved in. *Honeymoon* and *One More Honeymoon* were short-lived, but *Pre-Honeymoon*, by Alford Van Ronkel and Anne Williams (author of *Abie's Irish Rose*), was a big enough hit to move from the Lyceum to the Little.

In 1936, Sir Cedric Hardwicke made his U.S. debut in *Promise*. In 1937, when Cornelia Otis Skinner opened her one-woman show, *Edna, His Wife*, the house reverted to being called the Little. A sparkling revue, *Reunion in New York*, opened in 1940 and reunited a group of talented performers from Vienna who had been introduced to New Yorkers previously in another review, *From Vienna* (1939).

The Little Theatre ceased being a legitimate Broadway theatre for the next two decades. During this hiatus, the house, located adjacent to the headquarters of *The New York Times*, was known as The New York Times Hall from 1942 until 1959, when it became an ABC television studio.

The Little returned to the legitimate fold in 1963, with *Tambourines to Glory*, a gospel music play by Langston Hughes, the American jazz poet, novelist, playwright, activist and columnist, and Jobe Huntly. The Paul Taylor Dance Company played there in the same year. In 1964, Habimah, the national theatre of Israel, staged *The Dybukk*, *Children of the Shadows*, and *Each had Wings*. Later that year, Paul Newman, Joanne Woodward, and James Costigan appeared in the Actor's Studio production of Costigan's comedy, *Baby Want a Kiss*. The critics gave it the kiss of death.

In 1964, when the Pulitzer Prize-winning play *The Subject was Roses*, moved to the Little Theatre from the Royale, the theatre's name was changed to the Winthrop Ames after its founder. In March 1965, the name went back to the Little, which it retained until 1983.

From late 1964 to mid-1974, the theatre was leased to Westinghouse

Broadcasting and hosted the David Frost and the Merv Griffin TV shows. Fans of the latter program may remember announcer Arthur Treacher's cheery opening: "From the Little Theatre in Times Square, it's the Merv Griffin Show!"

In 1974, the Little went legit again and housed Ray Aranha's play, *My Sister, My Sister*. *The Runner Stumbles* (1976) was a success, but *Unexpected Guests* (1977) was a failure. *Lamppost Reunion*, Louis LaRusso II's much-heralded play about a Frank Sinatra-like singer returning to his old haunts in Hoboken, New Jersey, managed a run of only 77 performances.

In June 1977, Albert Innaurato's comedy, *Gemini*, moved in, and it epitomized the kind of show Winthrop Ames wanted in his theatre. The play was first done at Playwright's Horizons, then at the PAF Playhouse in Huntington, Long Island, followed by a production at the Circle Repertory Company. Finally, this production was moved to the Little, where it ran for an amazing 1,788 performances, making it the Little's longest-running show to that time, and the fourth-longest-running non-musical play in Broadway history.

My partner, Donald Tick, and I purchased the Little Theatre in 1979. In 1981, after the show closed that had been running at the theatre when we purchased it, we spent a considerable amount to restore the house. The interior was beautifully redesigned by ADCA Design.

As earlier described, my first three bookings at the theatre as the new owner did not fare well. They were *Ned and Jack* (1981), William Alfred's *The Curse of an Aching Heart* (1982) starring Faye Dunaway, and *Solomon's Child* (1982), an expose of fanatical religious cults.

In June 1982, only two years after we began bringing plays to the Little Theatre, our first unexpected hit play came to the house. It was *Torch Song Trilogy* by Harvey Fierstein, who starred in his own trio of bittersweet comedies about gay life.

The triptych originally played at La MaMa E.T.C. It was next done at the Richard Allen Center for Culture. Then it appeared at the Actors' Playhouse before moving to the Little Theatre.

Sample Broadway Musical Production and Operating Budgets; Sample Recoupment Schedules

2015 Sample Production Budgets

BROADWAY MUSICAL PRODUCTION BUDGETS
FOR DEVELOPMENT, OUT OF TOWN AND BROADWAY TRANSFER

ESTIMATED TOTAL PRODUCTION CAPITALIZATION $12,750,000

ESTIMATED DEVELOPMENT COSTS		
Developmental Expenses	$ 140,000	
Dance Pre-Production	$ 15,000	
TOTAL DEVELOPMENT COSTS		**$ 155,000**

ESTIMATED PRODUCTION COSTS - OUT OF TOWN		
PHYSICAL PRODUCTION	$ 2,198,760	
PRODUCTION FEES - CREATIVE STAFF	$ 724,951	
PRODUCTION FEES - PRODUCTION STAFF	$ 296,875	
ADVERTISING & PUBLICITY	$ 85,000	
REHEARSAL AND NY COMPANY TECH SALARIES	$ 1,304,902	
PRE-PRODUCTION & TECH EXPENSES	$ 1,464,446	
GENERAL & ADMINISTRATIVE COSTS	$ 147,000	
TOTAL PRODUCTION COSTS - OUT OF TOWN		**$ 6,221,934**

ESTIMATED PRODUCTION COSTS - BROADWAY ENGAGEMENT		
PHYSICAL PRODUCTION	$ 373,500	
PRODUCTION FEES - CREATIVE STAFF	$ 196,850	
PRODUCTION FEES - PRODUCTION STAFF	$ 46,875	
ADVERTISING & PUBLICITY PRODUCTION COSTS	$ 100,000	
NY ADVERTISING & PUBLICITY	$ 1,165,000	
REHEARSAL AND NY COMPANY TECH SALARIES	$ 764,091	
PRE-PRODUCTION & TECH EXPENSES	$ 1,495,527	
GENERAL & ADMINISTRATIVE COSTS	$ 29,234	
TOTAL PRODUCTION COSTS - BROADWAY ENGAGEMENT		**$ 4,171,077**

SECURITY BONDS & ROYALTY ADVANCES		
Actors Equity Association	$ 289,438	
IATSE	$ 17,500	
ATPAM	$ 11,860	
Adaptor	$ 10,000	
Authors	$ 60,000	
Director	$ 43,192	
Choreographer	$ 20,000	
Scenic Designer	$ -	

Costume Designer	$	-	
Lighting Designer	$	-	
Sound Designer	$	-	
TOTAL SECURITY BONDS & ROYALTY ADVANCES		$	**451,989**
CONTINGENCY & RESERVE		$	**-**
TOTAL MINIMUM CAPITAL REQUIRED		$	**11,000,000**
CONTINGENCY & RESERVE		$	**1,750,000**
TOTAL MAXIMUM CAPITAL REQUIRED		$	**12,750,000**

2015 Sample Broadway Musical Production Budgets

ESTIMATED OUT OF TOWN PRODUCTION COSTS $6,221,934

PHYSICAL PRODUCTION

Scenery, Scenic Electrics & Automation Prep	$ 900,000	
Props	$ 150,000	
Costumes & Shoes	$ 495,000	
Understudy Costumes & Shoes	$ 105,000	
Wigs & Hair (incl U/S)	$ 66,000	
Makeup & Prosthetics	$ 2,500	
Electrics - Preparation Charge	$ 65,000	
Electrics - Perishables	$ 37,500	
Sound - Preparation	$ 52,500	
Sound - Perishables	$ 35,000	
Projections - Preparation Charge	$ -	
Custom Rigging & Chain Motor Rental	$ 45,000	
Tools, Hardware, Rolling Stock	$ 25,000	
Departmental Expenses	$ 80,000	
Musical Instruments	$ 25,000	
Sales/Use Tax	$ 115,260	
		$ 2,198,760

PRODUCTION FEES - CREATIVE STAFF

Authors	$ 50,000
Underlying Rights	$ -
Adaptor	$ 15,000
Director	$ 21,599
Asst Director	$ 15,000
Choreographer	$ 30,750
Asst Choreographer	$ 18,500
Scenic Designer	$ 30,000
Assoc Scenic Designer	$ 34,650
Assistant Scenic Designer(s)	$ 23,552
Costume Designer	$ 30,000
Assoc Costume Designer	
	$ 34,650
Assistant Costume Designer(s)	$ 23,552

Lighting Designer	$	30,000
Assoc Lighting Designer	$	23,400
Assistant Lighting Designer(s)	$	23,552
Sound Designer	$	18,750
Assoc Sound Designer	$	17,600
Projection Designer	$	-
Hair Designer	$	7,500
Assistant Hair Designer	$	3,750
Make-Up Designer	$	3,750
Orchestrator	$	75,000
Music Copying	$	55,000
Transcription	$	-
Musial Director - pre-production	$	10,000
Vocal Arranger	$	10,000
Dance Music Arranger	$	10,000
Synthesizer Programmer	$	12,000
Company Payroll Taxes	$	42,205
Company Union Fringe Benefits	$	55,191
	$	724,951

PRODUCTION FEES - PRODUCTION STAFF

General Manager	$	43,125
Casting Director	$	26,250
Production Managers	$	45,000
Company Press Agent	$	15,375
Company Marketing Director	$	13.125
Production Legal Fee	$	130,000
Accounting Fees	$	24,000
	$	296,875

ADVERTISING & PUBLICITY PRODUCTION COSTS

"B"-Roll Production Costs		
Artwork, Mechanicals & Typesetting		
Printing	$	85,000
Internet & Website		
TV & Radio Production		
Photography		
	$	85,000

OOT ADVERTISING & PUBLICITY

OOT Pre-Opening Print Advertising	
OOT Pre-Opening TV & Radio Advertising	
OOT Pre-Opening Outdoor Advertising	
OOT Pre-Opening Direct Mail Advertising	
OOT Group Sales Promotions	$
OOT Front-of-House-Displays	

OOT Publicity, Promotion & Marketing
OOT Post-Opening Additional Advertising
OOT Press Expenses & Miscellaneous

$

REHEARSAL AND OOT COMPANY TECH SALARIES

Principals	6		$	75,894
Ensemble	12	$ 151,788		
Swings	4	$ 53,126		
Production Stage Manager	1	$ 32,690		
Assistant Stage Manager	1	$ 18,768		
2nd Assistant Stage Manager	1	$ 14,700		
Dance Captain Premium		$ 4,337		
New Media Fee		$ 7,228		
Equity Vacation Pay		$ 14,341		
Equity Sick Leave		$ 11,204		
AEA Buyouts		$ -		
Shop Crew (Preparation)		$ 50,000		
Company Crew (Preparation & Take-in)		$ 150,000		
Company Crew (Rehearsals to 1st Preview)		$ 100,000		
Wardrobe Supervisor (Preparation & Take-in)		$ 10,000		
Wardrobe Supervisor (Rehearsals to 1st Preview)		$ 12,000		
Dressers (Rehearsals to 1st Preview)		$ 45,000		
Hairdresser (Preparation & Take-in)		$ 3,600		
Hairdresser (Rehearsals to 1st Preview)		$ 12,000		
Moving Lights Programmer (Preparation & Take-in)		$ 7,500		
Moving Lights Programmer (Rehearsals through Preview)		$ 25,000		
Projection Programmer		$ -		
Musical Director		$ 24,500		
Rehearsal Musicians (NY studio to 1st orch reh)		$ 40,000		
Company Musicians (Orchestra Rehearsals)		$ 47,120		
Company Manager & Asst		$ 38,918		
General Manager		$ 51,750		
Production Manager		$ 4,800		
Company Press Agent		$ 11,600		
Production Assistant		$ 5,600		
Orchestra Contractor		$ 5,500		
Company Payroll Taxes		$ 119,573		
Company Union Fringe Benefits		$ 156,365		
			$	1,304,902

PRE-PRODUCTION & TECH EXPENSES

Cast Album	$	-
Design Studio Expenses, Models, Blueprints	$	50,000
Casting & Audition Expenses	$	15,000
Rehearsal Hall	$	45,000
Transportation, Hotel & Per Diem	$	517,446
IATSE Hotel & Per Diem	$	12,000
Local Hauling	$	65,000

Truck Loaders - Take-in	$ 15,000	
Local Stagehands - Advance thru focus	$ 350,000	
Local Stagehands - Cast On-Stage to 1st preview	$ 250,000	
Local Stagehands - Rehearsals during previews	$ 125,000	
Preliminary Theatre Rent & Expenses	$ -	
Opening Night	$ 20,000	
		$ 1,464,446

GENERAL & ADMINISTRATIVE COSTS

Office Fees	$ 27,000	
Executive Producer	$ 27,000	
Insurance	$ 75,000	
Legal Expenses/Filing Fees	$ 5,000	
Office Operating Costs	$ 5,000	
Computer Payroll Service	$ 3,000	
Miscellaneous & Other	$ 5,000	
		$ 147,000

TOTAL ESTIMATED OUT OF TOWN PRODUCTION COSTS $ 6,221,934

2015 Sample Broadway Musical Production Budgets

ESTIMATED BROADWAY TRANSFER
PRODUCTION COSTS $4,171,077

PHYSICAL PRODUCTION		
Scenery, Scenic Electrics & Automation Prep	$	100,000
Props	$	20,000
Costumes & Shoes	$	18,000
Understudy Costumes & Shoes	$	4,000
Wigs & Hair (incl U/S)	$	6,000
Makeup & Prosthetics	$	500
Electrics - Preparation Charge	$	30,000
Electrics - Perishables	$	10,000
Sound - Preparation	$	30,000
Sound - Perishables	$	20,000
Projections - Preparation Charge	$	-
Custom Rigging & Chain Motor Rental	$	30,000
Tools, Hardware, Rolling Stock	$	25,000
Departmental Expenses	$	80,000
Musical Instruments	$	-
Sales/Use Tax	$	-
	$	373,500

PRODUCTION FEES - CREATIVE STAFF		
Authors	$	-
Underlying Rights	$	-
Adaptor	$	-
Director	$	7,200
Asst Director	$	9,000
Choreographer	$	10,250
Asst Choreographer	$	11,100
Scenic Designer	$	10,000
Assoc Scenic Designer	$	8,250
Assistant Scenic Designer(s)	$	5,888
Costume Designer	$	10,000
Assoc Costume Designer	$	8,250

Assistant Costume Designer(s)	$	5,888
Lighting Designer	$	10,000
Assoc Lighting Designer	$	12,600
Assistant Lighting Designer(s)	$	17,664
Sound Designer	$	6,250
Assoc Sound Designer	$	11,200
Projection Designer	$	-
Hair Designer	$	2,500
Assistant Hair Designer	$	1,250
Make-Up Designer	$	1,250
Orchestrator	$	10,000
Music Copying	$	7,500
Transcription	$	-
Musical Director - pre-production	$	-
Vocal Arranger	$	-
Dance Music Arranger	$	-
Synthesizer Programmer	$	-
Company Payroll Taxes	$	13,351
Company Union Fringe Benefits	$	17,459
	$	196,850

PRODUCTION FEES - PRODUCTION STAFF

General Manager	$	14,375
Casting Director	$	8,750
Production Managers	$	15,000
Company Press Agent	$	4,375
Company Marketing Director	$	4,375
Production Legal Fee	$	-
Accounting Fees	$	-
	$	46,875

ADVERTISING & PUBLICITY PRODUCTION COSTS

"B"-Roll Production Costs		
Artwork, Mechanicals & Typesetting		
Printing	$	100,000
Internet & Website		
TV & Radio Production		
Photography		
	$	100,000

NY ADVERTISING & PUBLICITY

NY Pre-Opening Print Advertising		
NY Pre-Opening TV & Radio Advertising		
NY Pre-Opening Outdoor Advertising		
NY Pre-Opening Direct Mail Advertising		
NY Group Sales Promotions	$	1,165,000
NY Front-of-House Displays		

NY Publicity, Promotion & Marketing
NY Post-Opening Additional Advertising
NY Press Expenses & Miscellaneous

$ 1,165,000

REHEARSAL AND NY COMPANY TECH SALARIES

Principals	6	$	43,368
Ensemble	12	$	86,736
Swings	4	$	30,358
Production Stage Manager	1	$	13,076
Assistant Stage Manager	1	$	9,384
2nd Assistant Stage Manager	1	$	7,840
Dance Captain Premium		$	2,168
New Media Fee		$	2,711
Equity Vacation Pay		$	7,826
Equity Sick Leave		$	6,114
AEA Buyouts		$	-
Shop Crew (Preparation)		$	6,000
Company Crew (Preparation & Take-in)		$	120,000
Company Crew (Rehearsals to 1st Preview)		$	45,000
Wardrobe Supervisor (Preparation & Take-in)		$	5,000
Wardrobe Supervisor (Rehearsals to 1st Preview)		$	5,000
Dressers (Rehearsals to 1st Preview)		$	35,000
Hairdresser (Preparation & Take-in)		$	3,000
Hairdresser (Rehearsals to 1st Preview)		$	9,000
Moving Lights Programmer (Preparation & Take-in)		$	7,500
Moving Lights Programmer (Rehearsals through Preview)		$	22,500
Projection Programmer		$	-
Musical Director		$	14,000
Rehearsal Musicians (NY studio to 1st orch reh)		$	18,000
Company Musicians (Orchestra Rehearsals)		$	47,120
Company Manager & Asst		$	14,152
General Manager		$	23,000
Production Manager		$	4,800
Company Press Agent		$	11,600
Production Assistant		$	4,800
Orchestra Contractor		$	-
Company Payroll Taxes		$	68,917
Company Union Fringe Benefits		$	90,122

$ 764,091

PRE-PRODUCTION & TECH EXPENSES

Design Studio Expenses, Models, Blueprints	$	2,500
Casting & Audition Expenses	$	-
Rehearsal Hall	$	15,000
Star Per Diem & Living	$	16,000
Author Transportation	$	10,000

Author Per Diem & Living	$	13,125
Transportation, Hotel & Per Diem	$	20,000
IATSE Hotel & Per Diem	$	25,000
Local Hauling	$	65,000
Truck Loaders - Take-in	$	30,000
Local Stagehands	$	800,000
Preliminary Theatre Rent & Expenses	$	348,902
Opening Night	$	150,000
		$ 1,495,527

GENERAL & ADMINISTRATIVE COSTS

Office Fees	$	12,000
Executive Producer	$	12,000
Insurance	$	-
Legal Expenses/Filing Fees	$	-
Office Operating Costs	$	1,000
Computer Payroll Service	$	1,200
Miscellaneous & Other	$	3,034
	$	29,234

**TOTAL ESTIMATED BROADWAY
TRANSFER PRODUCTION COSTS**   **$ 4,171,077**

2015 Sample Musical Pre-Broadway Estimated Fixed Weekly Operating Budget

PRE-BROADWAY OUT OF TOWN OPERATING COSTS

SALARIES

Star			$ 4,500
Principals	5		$ 22,500
Ensemble	12		$ 21,684
Swings	4		$ 7,589
		PSM	$ 3,669
Stage Managers		SM	$ 2,346
		ASM	$ 1,960
Dance Captain Premium			$ 496
Principal Understudy Assignments			$ 396
Chorus specialites			$ 400
Chorus specialty covers			$ 300
X-risk			$ 280
New Media Fee			$ 904
Equity Vacation Pay			$ 2,458
Equity Sick Leave			$ 1,920
Production Crew	4		$ 1,600
Company Crew	7		$ 15,400
Wardrobe Supervisor	1		$ 1,900
Wardrobe Asst Sup	1		$ 1,700
Star Dressers	1		$ 1,700
Wardrobe Dressers	0		$ -
Hairdresser & Assistants	1		$ 1,650
Musical Director	1		$ 3,500
Company Musicians	3		$ 6,000
Company Manager & Assistant	2		$ 3,538
Company Payroll Taxes			$ 14,156
Company Union Fringe Benefits			$ 18,511
			$ 141,056

WEEKLY FIXED ROYALTIES, FEES & EXPENSES

General Manager	$ 5,750
Press Agent	$ -
Marketing Firm	$ 2,500
Production Manager	$ 1,200
Music Supervisor	$ -
Orchestra Contractor	$ 931
Vocal Arranger	$ 350
Dance Music Arranger	$ 350
Casting Director	$ 1,200
Hair Designer	$ 400

Rehearsals & Work Calls	$ -		
Transportation & Living	$ 43,400		
Star Car Service	$ 1,600		
		$ 57,681	

DEPARTMENTAL EXPENSES

Carpenter, Automation & Props	$ 500		
Electrics & Sound	$ 1,250		
Wardrobe, Hair & Makeup	$ 2,500		
Company & Stage Managers	$ 750		
		$ 5,000	

EQUIPMENT RENTALS

Automation	$ 9,000		
Electrics & Moving Lights	$ 11,500		
Sound	$ 10,000		
Projections	$ -		
Genie Lifts & Chain Motors	$ 750		
		$ 31,250	

GENERAL & ADMINISTRATIVE

Office Fee	$ 3,000		
Executive Producer	$ 3,000		
Legal	$ 1,000		
Accounting	$ 1,935		
Insurance	$ 7,212		
Production Maintenance/Closing reserve	$ -		
Photocopying, Telefax, Phones, Postage	$ 250		
Computer Payroll Service	$ 380		
Miscellaneous & Other	$ 500		
		$ 17,277	

**TOTAL ESTIMATED PRE-BROADWAY OUT OF TOWN
COMPANY FIXED WEEKLY OPERATING COSTS**   **$ 252,263**

2015 Sample Broadway Musical
Estimated Fixed Weekly Operating Budget

BROADWAY OPERATING COSTS

SALARIES			
Star	2		$ 50,000
Principals	4		$ 20,000
Ensemble	12		$ 21,684
Swings	4		$ 6,837
		PSM	$ 3,061
Stage Managers		SM	$ 2,109
		ASM	$ 1,766
Dance Captain Premium			$ 496
Principal Understudy Assignments			$ 396
Chorus specialites			$ 380
Chorus specialty covers			$ 285
X-risk			$ 320
New Media Fee			$ 320
Equity Vacation Pay			$ 2,433
Equity Sick Leave			$ 1,901
Production Crew	4		$ 1,600
Company Crew	7		$ 15,400
Wardrobe Supervisor	1		$ 1,900
Wardrobe Asst Sup	1		$ 1,700
Star Dressers	1		$ 1,700
Wardrobe Dressers	5		$ 7,500
Hairdresser & Assistants	3		$ 4,650
Musical Director	1		$ 3,750
Company Manager & Assistant	2		$ 3,538
Company Payroll Taxes			$ 13,905
Company Union Fringe Benefits			$ 17,114
			$ 184,745

WEEKLY FIXED ROYALTIES, FEES & EXPENSES	
General Manager	$ 5,750
Press Agent	$ 2,750
Marketing Firm	$ 2,500
Production Manager	$ 1,200
Music Supervisor	$ -
Orchestra Contractor	$ 931
Vocal Arranger	$ 350
Dance Music Arranger	$ 350
Casting Director	$ 1,200
Hair Designer	$ 400
Rehearsals & Work Calls	$ 1,600

Star per diem & Living Expense	$ 7,500	
Star Car Service	$ 3,250	
		$ 27,781

ADVERTISING & PUBLICITY

Print Advertising		
Television & Radio Advertising		
Outdoor Advertising		
Direct Response		
Production, Artwork & Mechanicals	$ 100,000	
Publicity, Promotion & Marketing		
Website		
Online Media		
Broadcast Residuals		
Press Agent Expenses		
		$ 100,000

DEPARTMENTAL EXPENSES

Carpenter, Automation & Props	$ 500	
Electrics & Sound	$ 1,250	
Wardrobe, Hair & Makeup	$ 2,500	
Company & Stage Managers	$ 750	
		$ 5,000

EQUIPMENT RENTALS

Automation	$ 9,000	
Electrics & Moving Lights	$ 11,500	
Sound	$ 10,000	
Projections	$ -	
Genie Lifts & Chain Motors	$ 750	
		$ 31,250

THEATRE EXPENSES

Theatre Operating Expenses	$ 26,000	
Air Conditioning	$ 2,000	
House Manager	$ 2,342	
Box office	$ 10,992	
Porters & Cleaners	$ 6,188	
Ushers, Ticket Takers, Doorman	$ 10,928	
Theatre Stagehands	$ 34,650	
Rehearsals & Work Calls	$ 2,340	
Holiday Pay	$ 944	
Theatre Musicians	$ 31,702	
Theatre Payroll Tax Burden	$ 19,266	
		$ 147,352

GENERAL & ADMINISTRATIVE

Office Fee	$ 3,000	
Executive Producer	$ 3,000	

Legal	$	850
Accounting	$	1,935
Insurance	$	7,212
Production Maintenance/Closing reserve	$	5,000
Photocopying, Telefax, Phones, Postage	$	250
Computer Payroll Service	$	380
Miscellaneous & Other	$	500
		$ 22,127

TOTAL ESTIMATED BROADWAY COMPANY
FIXED WEEKLY OPERATING COSTS   **$ 518,254**

2015 Sample Recoupment Schedule

ESTIMATED PRE-BROADWAY OUT OF TOWN
<u>NO AMORTIZATION</u>

Percentage of Capacity:	40%	50%	60%	70%	Break Even 79%	90%	Capacity 100% Estimated
GROSS GROSS BOX OFFICE RECEIPTS	$ 354,912	$ 443,640	$ 532,368	$ 621,096	$ 702,726	$ 798,552	$ 887,280
Deductions (7.5%)	26,618	33,273	39,928	46,582	52,704	59,891	66,546
NET GROSS BOX OFFICE RECEIPTS	$ 328,294	$ 410,367	$ 492,440	$ 574,514	$ 650,021	$ 738,661	$ 820,734
LESS: WEEKLY OPERATING EXPENSES:							
Guarantee	$ 285,000	$ 285,000	$ 285,000	$ 285,000	$ 285,000	$ 285,000	$ 285,000
Royalty (10%)	$ 32,829	$ 41,037	$ 49,244	$ 57,451	$ 65,002	$ 73,866	$ 82,073
Theatre Expenses	$ 300,000	$ 300,000	$ 300,000	$ 300,000	$ 300,000	$ 300,000	$ 300,000
TOTAL EXPENSES	$ 617,829	$ 626,037	$ 634,244	$ 642,451	$ 650,002	$ 658,866	$ 667,073
TOTAL MONIES TO SPLIT	$ (289,536)	$ (215,670)	$ (141,804)	$ (67,938)	$ 19	$ 79,795	$ 153,661
50% Producer	$ -	$ -	$ -	$ -	$ 9.60	$39,897.27	$76,830.30
50% Presenter	$ -	$ -	$ -	$ -	$ 9.60	$39,897.27	$76,830.30
TOTAL COMPANY SHARE	$ 317,829	$ 326,037	$ 334,244	$ 342,451	$ 350,012	$ 398,763	$ 443,904
TOTAL WEEKLY OPERATING EXPENSES	$ 252,263	$ 252,263	$ 252,263	$ 252,263	$ 252,263	$ 252,263	$ 252,263
SURPLUS BEFORE ROYALTIES	$ 65,566	$ 73,773	$ 81,981	$ 90,188	$ 97,748	$ 146,500	$ 191,640
WEEKLY OPERATING PROFIT (POOL BASIS)	$ 65,566	$ 73,773	$ 81,981	$ 90,188	$ 97,748	$ 146,500	$ 191,640
LESS: Pool Royalties	$ 25,977	$ 29,229	$ 32,481	$ 35,733	$ 38,728	$ 58,043	$ 75,928
NET WEEKLY OPERATING PROFIT	$ 39,589	$ 44,544	$ 49,500	$ 54,456	$ 59,021	$ 88,457	$ 115,712
Total Amount Applied Toward Recoupment							
Amortization of Production Costs	$ -	$ -	$ -	$ -	$ -	$ -	$ -
Weekly Operating Profit	$ 39,589	$ 44,544	$ 49,500	$ 54,456	$ 59,021	$ 88,457	$ 115,712
NET PROFIT TOWARD RECOUPMENT	$ 39,589	$ 44,544	$ 49,500	$ 54,456	$ 59,021	$ 88,457	$ 115,712

2015 Sample Recoupment Schedule

ESTIMATED FOR 1200-SEAT BROADWAY THEATRE
<u>WITH AMORTIZATION</u>

Percentage of Capacity:	Weekly Breakeven 50.78%	60%	65%	70%	80%	90%	Capacity 100% Estimated
GROSS GROSS BOX OFFICE RECEIPTS	$ 659,734	$779,520	$ 844,480	$ 909,440	$ 1,039,360	$1,169,280	$ 1,299,200
Deductions	62,675	74,054	80,226	86,397	98,739	111,082	123,424
NET GROSS BOX OFFICE RECEIPTS	$ 597,059	$705,466	$ 764,254	$ 823,043	$ 940,621	$1,058,198	$ 1,175,776
LESS: WEEKLY OPERATING EXPENSES:							
Fixed Weekly Operating Expenses	$ 518,254	$518,254	$ 518,254	$ 518,254	$ 518,254	$ 518,254	$ 518,254
Theatre Percentage Rent	$ 41,794	$ 49,383	$ 53,498	$ 57,613	$ 65,843	$ 74,074	$ 82,304
Star Percentage	$ -	$ -	$ -	$ 2,304	$ 14,062	$ 31,640	$ 55,155
TOTAL WEEKLY OPERATING EXPENSES	$ 560,048	$567,637	$ 571,752	$ 578,172	$ 598,160	$ 623,968	$ 655,714
SURPLUS BEFORE ROYALTIES	$ 37,011	$137,829	$ 192,502	$ 244,872	$ 342,461	$ 434,231	$ 520,062
Amortization (Note #3)	$ 37,011	$137,829	$ 192,502	$ 210,960	$ 210,960	$ 210,960	$ 210,960
Reduction of Amortization	$ -	$ -	$ -	$ -	$ -	$ -	$ -
NET AMORTIZATION	$ 37,011	$137,829	$ 192,502	$ 210,960	$ 210,960	$ 210,960	$ 210,960
WEEKLY OPERATING PROFIT (POOL BASIS)	$ -	$ -	$ -	$ 33,911	$ 131,501	$ 223,270	$ 309,102
LESS: Pool Royalties (Note #2)	$ 37,000	$ 37,000	$ 37,000	$ 37,000	$ 52,101	$ 88,460	$ 122,466
NET WEEKLY OPERATING PROFIT	$ (37,000)	$(37,000)	$ (37,000)	$ (3,089)	$ 79,400	$ 134,811	$ 186,636
Total Amount Applied Toward Recoupment							
Amortization Of Production Costs	$ 37,011	$137,829	$ 192,502	$ 210,960	$ 210,960	$ 210,960	$ 210,960
Weekly Operating Profit	(37,000)	(37,000)	(37,000)	(3,089)	79,400	134,811	186,636
NET PROFIT TOWARD RECOUPMENT	$ 11	$100,829	$ 155,502	$ 207,872	$ 290,360	$ 345,771	$ 397,596
Number of weeks to recoup Production Costs	n/a	105	68	51	36	31	27

$10,548,011 (not including bonds, advances and reserves)

2015 Sample Recoupment Schedule

ESTIMATED FOR 1200-SEAT BROADWAY THEATRE
<u>NO AMORTIZATION</u>

Percentage of Capacity:	Weekly Breakeven 49.09%	60%	70%	75%	80%	90%	Estimated Capacity 100%
GROSS GROSS BOX OFFICE RECEIPTS	$637,777	$779,520	$909,440	$974,400	$1,039,360	$1,169,280	$1,299,200
Deductions	60,589	74,054	86,397	92,568	98,739	111,082	123,424
NET GROSS BOX OFFICE RECEIPTS	$577,188	$705,466	$823,043	$881,832	$940,621	$1,058,198	$1,175,776
LESS: WEEKLY OPERATING EXPENSES:							
Fixed Weekly Operating Expenses	$518,254	$518,254	$518,254	$518,254	$518,254	$518,254	$518,254
Theatre Percentage Rent	$40,403	$49,383	$57,613	$61,728	$65,843	$74,074	$82,304
Star Percentage	$ -	$ -	$2,304	$8,183	$14,062	$31,640	$55,155
TOTAL WEEKLY OPERATING EXPENSES	$558,657	$567,637	$578,172	$588,166	$598,160	$623,968	$655,714
SURPLUS BEFORE ROYALTIES	$18,531	$137,829	$244,872	$293,666	$342,461	$434,231	$520,062
WEEKLY OPERATING PROFIT (POOL BASIS)	$18,531	$137,829	$244,872	$293,666	$342,461	$434,231	$520,062
LESS: Pool Royalties	$18,500	$54,608	$97,018	$116,351	$135,683	$172,042	$206,049
NET WEEKLY OPERATING PROFIT	$31	$83,221	$147,854	$177,316	$206,778	$262,188	$314,014
Total Amount Applied Toward Recoupment							
Amortization Of Production Costs	$ -	$ -	$ -	$ -	$ -	$ -	$ -
Weekly Operating Profit	$31	$83,221	$147,854	$177,316	$206,778	$262,188	$314,014
NET PROFIT TOWARD RECOUPMENT	$31	$83,221	$147,854	$177,316	$206,778	$262,188	$314,014
Number of weeks to recoup Production Costs	n/a	127	71	59	51	40	34

$10,548,011 (not including bonds, advances and reserves)

CPSIA information can be obtained
at www.ICGtesting.com
Printed in the USA
BVHW082157110719
553262BV00001B/5/P